FATAL DESTINY
The Carjacking Murder of Dr. Pam Basu

James H. Lilley

© 2012 James H. Lilley
All rights reserved. No part of this book may be reproduced, stored in a retrieval system or transmitted in any form or by any means without the prior written permission of the publishers, except by a reviewer who may quote brief passages in a review to be printed in a newspaper, magazine or journal.

First printing.

Acknowledgements

My sincere thanks to Congressman Roscoe G. Bartlett for his kind assistance in helping me obtain materials valuable in the preparation and completion of this book.

To Howard County State's Attorneys Michael Rexrode and Joseph Murtha and former Howard County Executive and Chief of Police James N. Robey for their support in this endeavor, thank you. I'm indebted to the men and women of the Howard County Police Department, the Maryland State Police, and the Public Defender's Office and to those sources that chose to remain anonymous for their contributions of time and materials.

The following are just some of those who contributed to this book:

Howard County State's Attorneys Office:
Christine Gage
Howard County Public Defender's Office:
Carol Hanson
Samuel Truitt
From the Howard County Police Department:
Mr. R. C. Bartley
Brook Donovan
Jody Tookey
Lee Lachman
Tom Martin
From the Howard County Sheriff's Office
Sheriff Michael Chiuchiolo
From the Maryland State Police:
Michael Marinaro
Marc Price
Scott Richardson
Steve Proctor

Dedication

Dedicated to the memory of Doctor Pam Basu, devoted wife of Steve and loving mother of Sarina. To Pam's mother, Lajya Davar, to Steve and Sarina, everyone in the Basu and Davar families who have had to suffer through the tragic loss of a good wife, caring mother, loving daughter and sister.

From the National Center for Forensic Science:
Charles Lodcio
Folkemer Photo and Computer Center:
Charles MacGill
Computer Wizards:
Lien Duong
Dean Clark

Preface

The brutal death of Doctor Pam Basu and forcible taking of her car on September 8, 1992 is the singular incident, which defined carjacking. Her senseless killing was truly the murder reported around the world. From CBS, NBC, and ABC to CNN and FOX News, People and Time Magazines, her death touched off a media frenzy.

The outcry over Doctor Pam Basu's murder brought thunderous applause from members of her community when they were told the suspects could face the death penalty. But, the cries for justice continued, and her death became the catalyst for House Bill H.R. 4542, The Anti-Car Theft Act of 1992. President George H. W. Bush signed that bill into law in the presence of members of the International Association of Chiefs of Police on October 25, 1992.

The case continues to make national news, as suspects pursue appeals and challenge legislation and court rulings. The crime has been cited in the Baltimore Sun, Washington Post, New York Times, London Times, The Associated Press, Los Angeles Times, USA Today and others. The media has referred to the Basu carjacking as "the case that won't go away." The crime stands as a lead case cited in legal documents, court cases and dictionaries. It has been cited as a primary case in West's Encyclopedia of American Law and Webster's Online Dictionary.

Yet, this hideous killing held a double twist that seemed better suited to a Hollywood Thriller. Pam's husband, Steve, while videotaping her departure from their home with their daughter, captured the images of the two men who would moments later, brutally beat and drag to death his loving wife. And, she lived and died in a town called Savage, Maryland.

Comments by President George H. W. Bush

The killing of Doctor Pam Basu was such a senseless, brutal act it shocked even the President of the United States, George H. W. Bush. President Bush spoke of her death when he addressed the International Association of Chiefs of Police in Detroit, Michigan on October 25, 1992.

"Let me start with a story that most of the domestic chiefs have heard about, probably the kind of story you hear about every day, but one that just sickened Barbara and me when we saw it on the news. I believe it was almost a month ago. In broad daylight, in a neighborhood near Washington, D. C. a woman was forced from her car at a Stop sign by two men, who then drove off. But the woman got tangled in her seatbelt outside the car, or maybe she hung on. What mother wouldn't? You see her baby was locked inside. And that woman was dragged almost two miles before the thieves crushed her against a fence. And then they tossed her little baby out by the roadside like some piece of trash. And I know that on this special Sunday in this special audience I am preaching to the choir, but this sort of thing must provoke outrage. People who act like animals have no place in decent society, and they should go to jail and stay in jail. I strongly support you and your efforts to do just that."

Only hours passed before President George Bush made a statement when signing the Anti-car Theft Act of 1992. The death of Pam Basu was the catalyst for this bill.

"Today I am pleased to sign into law H.R. 4542, the Anti-car Theft act of 1992. This legislation is absolutely critical if we are to strike back against auto thieves and cajackers. These criminals who show no respect for the lives or property of law-abiding Americans must be punished in the strongest possible manner.

This bill makes armed carjacking a federal offense. The recent wave of these carjackings has made the need for action clear. The bill also seeks to sap the profit motive for auto theft. Last year in the United States auto thieves stole cars valued at eight billion dollars. H.R. 4542 creates a second federal crime: Operating or maintaining a chop shop to alter stolen cars for resale or reduce them to parts that can be resold.

It is my sincere hope that this legislation will reduce the level of auto thefts and carjackings. Thugs and criminals will now have to think twice about stealing a car. If not, they will pay a high price for their actions."

Prologue

Pam was a very focused and dedicated woman. We met when we were students, she at the University of Maryland, College Park, and I at Catholic University. I met her at a friend's house and was immediately drawn to her by her nature. She was very friendly and open, but also very serious about her work. Even though we were both Indian, we came from very different backgrounds. Her parents were well off and she could move in circles of influential people. I wasn't from that type of background, but we clicked only because I think we complimented each other. My fears and hesitations evaporated when I met her. Suddenly, life didn't have to be so serious and we were happy together. Pam and I were married on July 7, 1980.

She was very disciplined and very dedicated to her work and her family. She was also very innocent and almost childlike at times. It was very good to have her in my life, where I think I provided the stability and she was very much the organizer. It was Pam who put together our household, our home.

She wanted the marriage to work, even when we had to be separated because of our work. She was in Pittsburgh working for Alcoa, and I remained behind in the Washington area to work until I found a job in Pittsburgh.

Pam was highly respected and admired by her colleagues. It was at an office party that I found that she was held in such high esteem. She often arrived for work early, and stayed late into the night to complete a project. She was very focused, often completing one project and moving on to the next. She knew what she wanted to do.

At the same time she was continuing her studies, and I often wondered how she found the time to do both. I couldn't imagine what it was like for her to work the hours as she did and pursue her education. She took so much on to herself, often completing projects on her own while she studied. But that was Pam. And at home you would never know this, because she was such a different person.

Alcoa asked her to stay on and become a director of one of their laboratories, but she declined the offer. We moved here in 1988 and she took a job with W. R. Grace in Columbia, Maryland. Once she was organized and settled in there, we bought the house in Savage. She worked hard setting everything up in the house and making it a home.

It was also at this time that we began discussing having a child. But Pam had had a surgical procedure because of pain she was suffering. But after the surgery we learned that the complications were much more serious than we originally thought. So, the doctor's advice was to wait for a period of time before we started thinking about having a baby. That was the time we thought that maybe we could adopt a child.

We discussed adoption and once we decided to go ahead, Pam, in typical fashion, went all out. We did everything ourselves. We didn't have an adoption agency to help us. The only thing we had was an agency that completed a home study. Once that was concluded, we did everything ourselves but, as always, Pam did most of the work. That was the essence of Pam's life. She was very devoted to whatever task had to be done and would never be satisfied until it was finished.

She traveled to India and patiently went through the process (it took about a month and half just to complete the paperwork) of picking up Sarina and bringing her back to America. Although she was very dedicated to her work, she arranged her schedule to spend as much time as possible with Sarina. There was so much joy that this baby brought into our lives, and especially Pam's life. She would read to Sarina every day and as time passed she was teaching Sarina to read, and at such an early age.

There were times when I came home from work and would peek through the window and watch Pam with Sarina. They would be together in the kitchen, Pam talking to Sarina and Sarina with spaghetti sauce on her face, smiling and laughing. It was very obvious that Pam was so very, very happy and that happiness was found in this beautiful little girl. Looking through the window I saw and understood this very special bond—the love shared between them. There was so much love and laughter that it was almost like looking inside a fairytale and seeing a perfect dream come true.

        Steve Basu

James H. Lilley

One

The second week of a new school year was beginning as a gentle breeze whisked away the last of the gray clouds from the morning sky. The sun, climbing higher against a backdrop of brightening blue, was a welcome sight after a dreary, rainy Labor Day weekend.

Shortly before 8:00 AM Officer Jody Ann Tookey of the Howard County Police Department stopped her cruiser on the parking lot of the California Inn. "It was the last day of the shift," she would later say, "and I couldn't wait for it to be over. It had been a miserable weekend to work." She sipped a Diet Coke and watched the steady stream of cars, pickup trucks and minivans carrying workers and mothers with school-aged children pass by. She took a sip of her Coke and thought that at least the last day of her shift would be a beautiful day.

Little did she know that a series of events were already in motion that would draw people from various backgrounds and professions together for the sole purpose of relating a horrifying tale.

Several miles away on Interstate 95, a burgundy Cadillac driven by Rodney Eugene Solomon was sputtering to a stop. Solomon drifted the car from the fast lane of traffic on to the asphalt shoulder beside the grassy median. There the Cadillac stopped for good, out of gas and its right front fender protruding partially into the traffic lane.

Solomon and his front seat passenger, Bernard Eric Miller, got out of the car after telling the occupants in the back seat, Tony Angelo Williams and LaShawn Faye Smith, they were going for gas. The two men then walked through the median strip, crossed the northbound lanes of I-95 and entered the rest stop.

Grace Lagana, a receptionist for the Visitors and Information Center at the rest stop, arrived for work and parked her Chrysler Labaron Convertible at about 8:10 AM. As she got out of her car she noticed two young black males walking quickly toward her and thought they were going to ask for directions.

As they drew nearer Rodney Solomon put his right hand in his pocket and said, "Gimme your car keys or I'll blow your fuckin' head off."

Lagana shook her head saying, "You'll have to, because you can't have my car."

Solomon grabbed her and they began to struggle for possession of the car keys. During the fight Solomon forcibly took the keys from Lagana, breaking the key chain in the process. Having taken possession of the keys, Solomon turned his attention away from Lagana and went to the car where he gained entry through the driver's door.

Lagana now struggled with the second man, Bernard Eric Miller. She was screaming for help while she fought, hoping to get the attention of anyone in the area. Miller shoved her to the ground, ran to the car and entered by the passenger's door while Solomon tried to start the car. Solomon twisted and turned the key, but the car wouldn't start because he'd unknowingly inserted the trunk key into the ignition switch.

Michael Woods, who was nearby using a pay telephone, heard Grace Lagana's screams and turned to see Miller shove her to the ground. He dropped the telephone and began running to help her, screaming at Miller to leave her alone.

Solomon and Miller, seeing Woods running towards them jumped from the car and raced across the parking lot, vanishing into a wooded area that surrounded the rest stop. Woods continued to purse the two men for a short distance before stopping and returning to check on Grace Lagana.

While the attempted carjacking of Grace Lagana's vehicle was taking place in the rest stop, Trooper Kevin Ringgold of the Maryland State Police was pulling over to check on the Cadillac. When he approached the car he saw two people sleeping in the backseat.

"I woke them up and asked if they were okay," Ringgold said. "They advised that they'd run out of gas and the other occupants had gone for help."

While he was attempting to push the Cadillac from the traveled portion of I-95, he saw Michael Woods waving to him from the entrance to the northbound rest stop. He crossed the highway and was told of the attempted carjacking.

Solomon and Miller had continued their flight in a southerly direction, eventually making their way to Gorman Road. On Gorman Road they turned east, and when they reached the entrance to Forest Ridge Elementary School, they crossed the street and walked into a residential neighborhood.

They approached the residence of John Bryan and knocked on the front door. When he failed to respond to their knocking, they began ringing the doorbell. Bryan peeked through the curtains and saw Solomon and Miller standing at his front door.

He decided not to answer the door and a few moments later they stopped their knocking and ringing and walked away.

After closing the door to her home, Laura Becraft turned and saw two black males standing in the driveway talking with her son. She hurried to them and told her son, "Get in the car."

"I need to use your phone," Rodney Solomon said, stepping toward her. "It's an emergency. I'm lost."

"I'm leaving," Becraft said. "Try another home."

Becraft quickly got into her vehicle, locked the doors and drove to a neighbor's house on Jaclyn Court to pick up another child. After she put her son's schoolmate in the car she turned and saw the same two Black males who had confronted her at her house, walking from the rear of the home.

Immediately, both men rushed toward her with the larger of the two men, Rodney Solomon, grabbing for her car keys. He caught her wrist and snarled, "Gimme me your keys. I have a gun."

"No," Becraft screamed and pushed him away. "Get away from me," she yelled loudly. "There's a police officer over there," she added, thinking the School Crossing Guard was at the intersection of Jeanne Court and Gorman Road.

The two men stood still for a few moments as Laura Becraft backed away from them toward the house. Then they turned slowly and shuffled across the street where Solomon began walking backward and pointing at Becraft.

"I'm calling the police," she yelled at them.

"I'm sorry, lady," Solomon called to her while raising his arms in the air. With that Solomon and Miller continued up the street and disappeared.

Only minutes earlier, Teresa Giddings left her residence on Jennifer Court to walk her children to school. When she arrived at Gorman Road, across from the elementary school, she noticed that the School Crossing Guard was absent. She decided to stay there to help the children cross the street.

While she was helping children cross the street to the school, she heard a scream and saw two black males walking from the area of Jaclyn Court. They approached the crossing area at Gorman Road and stood to her left "talking and muttering" among themselves.

As the traffic flow on Gorman Road lessened, Giddings assisted a group of children in crossing the street. The two black males crossed with the children and began running east on Gorman Road when a school bell rang.

Teresa Giddings spoke briefly with Marianne Pfeiffer, the Principal of Forest Ridge Elementary School, about the absence of the crossing guard. Pfeiffer told Giddings she would assist the rest of the children in crossing the road.

Giddings was leaving the school to go home when she met Laura Becraft who began telling her about the two black males who had attempted to steal her car keys.

At that time Giddings said, "I heard what sounded like a woman screaming behind the houses on Jaclyn Court."

At 8:25 AM a police radio operator dispatched a call to Police Officer Charles Dittman for two suspicious subjects running east on Gorman Road, and another for the attempted theft on Jaclyn Court. He acknowledged the call, but told the dispatcher he was several miles away.

Officer Tookey, who had monitored the calls, told the dispatcher she was only a minute or two away and would investigate the incidents. She drove from the parking lot of the California Inn and proceeded west on Whiskey Bottom Road.

Two

In the Basu household, on Horsham Drive in Savage, Maryland, the air was charged with excitement. Tuesday, September 8, 1992 was to be the first day of preschool for 22-month old Sarina. Biswanth "Steve" Basu and Pam Basu, proud and loving parents of Sarina, had slept little during the night. The nervous anticipation of their daughter's first day of preschool would deny them sleep. Yet, their lack of restful sleep would surely go unnoticed throughout the day.

Steve Basu, a mechanical engineer, owned a small firm, which was employed to perform engineering and construction management for various government agencies.

Pam Basu, a research scientist, was employed by W. R. Grace and Company in Columbia, Maryland. She had received her Bachelor's Degree in chemistry from the University of Maryland in 1978, and her Master's Degree in surface chemistry from Virginia Polytechnic Institute in 1980. She later earned her Doctorate at the University of Pittsburgh.

Doctor Basu's work in air pollution control had received international attention. Her thesis was published in the *Journal of the American Chemical Society,* the field's most prestigious publication, and is respected by scientists in Europe and Japan, as well as the United States.

Pam Basu wanted to raise a child and when she completed her education she went to India to adopt a child. Her first attempt ended in failure, but she battled red tape and enlisted the aid of the State Department. On her second attempt she adopted Sarina.

Steve Basu, video camera in hand, was determined to record every precious moment of Sarina's big day, which he and Pam would proudly show for family and friends in the days to follow. He was going to videotape everything possible at their home, including the departure of Pam and Sarina for the school. He would then meet them at the school to film her arrival and entry to meet her classmates.

It was around 8:25 AM when Pam walked out the front door with Sarina, down the steps and to her 1990 BMW. Steve stood on the steps, with his video camera running, while his wife placed their daughter in the child's seat in the rear of the car.

At about the same time, Julie Panzeri, their next-door neighbor, was leaving for work. She saw Pam Basu putting Sarina in the back of the car and Steve standing on the steps of their home videotaping the event. Panzeri said, "I got into my car and began to back out of my parking space. I had to stop because a Black Male, about 5' 8" with no shirt was walking down the middle of the street. Another black male, thinner, was walking down the sidewalk behind him. I waited for the first black male to pass then I pulled out and left.

When I drove away, Pam was still in the process of getting into her car and Steve was still videotaping. I noticed that the two men were walking very slowly, because I had to wait a few seconds for the one without the shirt to get out of my way. And they did seem to be watching Pam, because the first black male's head was turned in her direction as he was walking."

As Pam drove away, Steve went back into the house to get the baby sitter to show her where to pick up Sarina later that day.

David Self was preparing to drive Tammy Rienstra and her children to the Forest Ridge Elementary School. When they went to his pickup truck David, Tammy and her son, Joseph, got in the front of the truck. Dale Hicks and Tammy's other son, Michael, got into the bed of the pickup. Self drove away from the residence and turned on to Horsham Drive. David Self stopped the truck almost immediately and called to Hicks.

Hicks stood up in the bed of the truck and heard a woman screaming. He looked out over top of the truck cab and saw a BMW stopped at the intersection of Horsham Drive and Knights Bridge Road. Hicks said that he saw two black males, one being about 5' 10" and 160 pounds, about 27 years of age with dark skin and short hair. The second he described as shorter, thinner and younger and he was standing beside the car.

"I stood up and heard screams coming from the BMW at the stop sign at Knights Bridge," he said. "The first guy was in the driver's window. This guy was punching the woman in the face with his fists. The second guy was standing at the driver's door and punching the woman also. They hit her a lot."

"I saw two black males beating a woman inside a car at the corner of Knights Bridge and Horsham," Tammy Rienstra said. "Both of them were punching her from outside the driver's side of the car."

It was at this same time that Kevin Brown, a driver for the H. W. Jennings Trucking Company, was driving a dump truck on Knights Bridge Road approaching Horsham Drive. "I was driving out Knights Bridge toward Gorman Road at about 8:30," Brown said. "When I passed the intersection of Horsham Drive I noticed a BMW stopped at the Stop Sign at Knights Bridge and Horsham. What drew my attention to the car was, I saw a black male hanging inside the driver's window. The entire upper body of this guy was inside the car through the driver's window. I heard a woman scream from inside the car and I think I heard her yell, 'my baby. My baby.'"

"I stopped my truck in the road," Brown said. "I then looked in the rear view mirrors of the truck and saw a second black guy in the middle of the road near the island. I started to drift back through the intersection and when I got to the other side I stopped my truck. Before I got stopped, the second black Male started to run toward the BMW. He ran like he was running across a football field. This guy ran right to the car and opened the passenger's door. At this point I was getting out of my truck. The woman was laying across the front seat. I could see her legs on the passenger's side of the car. The guy on the driver's side was hitting her repeatedly with his fist. He was hitting her hard with full swings. He was coming out of left field with his swings, reaching way back to hit her.

I had taken a couple of steps away from my truck and then stopped. I was afraid of going up against both of those guys, so I went back to my truck to get a chain to even things out. It was very obvious this woman needed help. As I walked across the road, I saw the second guy kicking the woman out of the car from the passenger's side of the car. At the same time, the other guy had grabbed the woman up under her arms and was pulling her out of the car. He dropped her on the road and stepped over her to get in the driver's seat. I was about 12 paces away from the car at this point. The car starts to pull away. The driver's door is still open. The woman is laying on the road on her left side, reaching into the car with her left arm. I couldn't see what she grabbed on to. The car is now passing me. The driver slammed the driver's door. It looked like the car door closed on her arm somewhere around the wrist or forearm. At this point the woman was dragging on the road."

Brown paused for a moment and went on. "The car picked up speed quickly and drove away. The woman was hanging out of the car just flopping around. I saw parts of her hair laying on the road. I saw her strike the back of her head on the road real hard. When the car went out of sight I got in my truck and tried to follow. I could see what looked like a blood trail on the road where the car went down the street. By the time I got to Horsham Drive and Gorman Road the car was out of sight. There I saw another patch of hair."

Robert Hicks said, "The woman was screaming and fighting. She shot out of the car and landed on her rear end first. She jumped up and reached towards the car. The car took off slow, and the woman ran for a while. She tried to raise her feet and hold on, but the car hit a dip. She drops her feet and she flips. She hits feet first and then flips all around, flopping around like a fish—a rag doll. All the time she's screaming. Her head must have hit the ground because there was hair all over the place."

Catherine Nehring had stopped for the Stop Sign at Horsham Drive and Gorman Road when the BMW approached her car from behind. "It was about 8:25 AM when I left home for Forest Ridge Elementary School," she said. "I was waiting at the Stop Sign for traffic to clear when a car cut around me to the left and crossed Gorman Road. I saw the body dragging from the driver's side at that time. When I turned left on Gorman Road, I saw the car pull half way on to the right shoulder of the road. A man got out of the driver's seat, walked around the front of the car and opened the passenger's side rear door. He appeared to be trying to get something out of the car. He then pulled a baby's seat, with a toddler in it, out of the car and threw it on the road. The baby seat landed upright, but tipped over with the impact. The man got back into the driver's seat and sped off.

I yelled to another car that stopped to try to catch the car and get a license plate number. I then picked up the girl and put her in my car. After placing the baby's seat in the trunk I drove home, and on the way home I noticed human hair on Horsham Drive.

The man who got out of the car was black, about 30 years old, average height, with very short, dark curly hair. I don't believe he had any facial hair."

Keith McLamb, who also saw the BMW pull to the shoulder of Gorman Road said, "There was a scuffle in the back seat and then they threw the baby and car seat on the side of the street. They just took off with the lady still hanging on the car."

The BMW continued traveling west on Gorman Road. A car being driven eastbound by Guindalina Murphy passed the BMW. Mrs. Murphy saw what she believed was a body hanging on the driver's side of the car. "The driver had to know there was a person hanging on the side of the car," she said. Mrs. Murphy remembered seeing a police officer on the parking lot of the California Inn, turned around and proceeded back to report what she had seen. When she arrived the officer was gone.

People were continuing to come and go from Forest Ridge Elementary School. Sandra Benz had walked a short distance from the school and was standing at Falling Waters Road and Gorman Road. "I had stopped to look and listen for traffic before crossing. I heard a car accelerating at a very high speed towards me. I turned to my left to watch the car go by, when I noticed the look on the face of a woman who was walking on the opposite sidewalk going toward Route One. She was an Oriental woman and she was screaming something at the car. I quickly looked at the car, noticing that it was a light colored BMW. The reason I knew it was a BMW was that I recognized the symbol that appears on their cars. As the car sped by me doing at least 50 miles per hour, the Oriental woman was still screaming at the car. Then I noticed what I thought was a dummy attached to the driver's side of the car. My first thought was 'Gee, that's an awful expensive car for some kids to be driving to school, playing a joke like this.' The scene was just too unreal to believe. The woman was bouncing up and down as the car sped along, not slowing down, but going faster. I couldn't figure out how the woman was attached to the car and I was surprised that she wasn't going under the rear driver's wheel.

As I watched the car continue down Gorman Road I saw Stephanie Donnelly on the other side of the street. She was also waving and shouting to the car as it drove by. After the car was out of sight, I quickly turned and yelled to the Oriental lady that it must have been a joke and that wasn't a real person. She was crying and saying, 'No, that was a woman.'"

"I crossed Gorman Road and Stephanie Donnelly was walking toward me. When I asked her if that was a dummy or a real person, she said it was a real person because as the car drove by her, hair blew at her feet and she saw blood. We both stood there in shock and the Oriental woman just kept walking down the street shaking her head and crying."

Stephanie Donnelly had dropped her daughter off at Forest Ridge Elementary School and crossed the street to return home. "I saw a car coming down Gorman Road toward me. The car was traveling pretty fast, about 50 miles per hour. I was facing the driver's side of the car and I saw a body attached to it. At first, I didn't know it was a body. I thought it was maybe straw stuffed clothing, but as the car got closer to me the clothing was coming off of the rear end of the—of what I then knew to be a person. The whole rear end was exposed and I could tell that it was flesh. The feet were dragging on the ground. The feet were the only thing touching the road. It looked to me that the arm was kind of in the door, somewhere between the elbow and the shoulder. Right after the car passed me some hair blew up right—it stopped in the grass right at my feet. It was—it looked like a tumbleweed might look. I actually picked it up because I still couldn't believe that this was a person attached to this car. So I picked it up to see if it was really hair, and it was, no doubt in my mind. It was black and it was very loosely balled. I screamed, 'Oh my, God, stop. Stop. Oh, my God.' The car just kept going at the same speed and eventually crossed over 95."

It was only seconds later that Officer Tookey braked to a stop at the intersection of Stephens Road and Gorman Road. "At that time a white Female, who was crying, ran up to me. She advised that a Gold BMW was traveling down Gorman Road towards Columbia dragging a woman. She also stated that a child had been thrown from the car. At this point I started down Gorman road towards Columbia, and while driving along Gorman Road I observed drag marks on the roadway surface."

Jacqueline Hill, a school bus driver, had pulled off the road between Stephens Road and I-95 to check her bus for cleanliness. "I heard a noise that sounded like garbage cans clanging. I saw a gold colored car going west on Gorman road at about 55 to 60 miles per hour. When the car passed I saw a body being dragged by the car."

Officer Tookey stopped beside the bus and asked Hill if she had seen the vehicle. Hill, who was crying, was unable to speak and answered Officer Tookey's question by nodding and pointing west.

"As I continued west, and just over the I-95 overpass, I saw bloodstained clothing lying in the road," Officer Tookey said. "I kept heading west, and at a distance some 1500 feet from the overpass, I discovered a body lying face down in the roadway. The body was nude below the waist, and the clothing on the top half of the body was torn. The woman had a large hole in the top of her head and several cuts about the body."

Officer Tookey spoke to a witness who said he was behind the car. "They just took the body off the car and left. There were two Black males in the car and I think it was a foreign car of some kind."

Officer Tookey remained at the location with the body and informed other officers that the vehicle was still traveling in a westerly direction on Gorman Road. As more people began to arrive at her location, she asked that the road be closed to preserve evidence and prevent others from entering the crime scene. She asked for a supervisor and additional officers to respond to the area to assist her and then began writing down names and addresses of witnesses.

At one point she stopped what she was doing, walked to her car and removed a yellow plastic emergency blanket. She covered the body and later said, "I just couldn't let people see the woman lying there like that."

Three

Steve Basu and the babysitter left the family residence only minutes after Pam. He stopped for the Stop Sign at Horsham Drive and Knights Bridge and noticed a woman's shoe in the middle of the road. He turned to the babysitter and said, "It's kind of strange that a shoe is there." But he passed it off and drove on.

At Horsham Drive and Gorman he looked to his left and saw a group of women. "It seemed like there was—that something was going on." However not wanting to be late arriving at the school, he made a right turn on Gorman Road and proceeded east toward U. S. Route One.

"When we arrived at the school, Pam hadn't arrived there yet and I was—I was a little surprised because she's usually very punctual about these things. So I went inside and I asked the school principal if Pam and Sarina were here. And everybody said 'No' they hadn't come in yet. I said, 'We'll, wait ten or fifteen minutes.' I waited for only five or six minutes and then I said, 'I'll go back and see if there's something wrong with the car or whatever.' I asked my babysitter to wait there.

I came out of the parking lot and just kind of drove back the same way I came on 32, looking out for the car. I didn't see it.

I came all the way down to where 32 goes around into Route One. I turned around and came back to the school, hoping they might be there by then. When I got there they still had not arrived. So I got worried that maybe the car had broken down, or maybe Sarina—or something—and she'd decided to go home. I went back the same route again, this time driving slow and looking everywhere."

As Steve Basu searched for his wife and daughter, Officer Brook Donovan was on his way to Catherine Nehring's home to take a report regarding the child that was thrown from the car. Donovan said, "She was nervous—upset and had difficulty describing the event."

Officer Donovan looked the child over and saw no evidence of external injuries; however as a precaution, he requested an ambulance respond to the residence and had the child examined by EMS personnel.

When Donovan left the residence he went to the intersection of Horsham Drive and Gorman Road. "I discovered two clumps of black hair and a trail of blood going west on Gorman Road." He secured the location to protect and preserve the evidence.

Steve Basu's search went on. "When I came down 32 the second time I was driving real slow to look for her car. I thought maybe the car had broken down. When I didn't see the car on 32, I got off on Route One. And, again driving slowly on Route One, I went up to Gorman Road. I still didn't see the car. Then I decided to go home. I thought maybe something had happened—that Sarina got sick, or whatever and they went home. So I turned on to Gorman Road going towards the house. As I approached Horsham Drive I turned left and I saw… There was a police car parked on the other side of the street and I knew something was wrong right then. I slowed down and I asked the policeman if he had seen my wife and Sarina in the car. He told me to pull over and park behind him—and my heart just sank. I knew that something bad must have happened."

"After speaking with the man I knew he was the victim's husband," Officer Brook Donovan said. "My heart raced and I needed a few seconds to get my breath. I was going to make my first death notification and I wasn't sure what to say or how to say it. In fact, I wasn't even certain of the details surrounding her death. I informed him of his wife's death, but I'm not sure of exactly what I said to him."

Although Officer Donovan had asked that a supervisor be sent to his location to assist him in making the death notification, none were released from their assigned duties to help him.

"When I first looked at him I could tell that he knew something was terribly wrong," Donovan said. "After I told him his wife was dead… At first he looked confused. Then he started crying. For a while he kind of went back and forth between the two stages. Confusion. Crying.

A few minutes after telling him, I escorted Mr. Basu to Catherine Nehring's house so he could be with his daughter."

Four

Initially the calls received by the 911 Operator seemed to indicate the incident was a fatal hit and run traffic accident rather than a homicide. For that reason members of the Howard County Police Department's Traffic Enforcement Section were dispatched to the scene. One of the responding officers was Patrolman First Class Fred VonBriesen.

"I responded to the area of Gorman Road to assist Officers Jack Mitchell and Scott Wichtendahl. When I arrived on the scene I found that the officers were on Gorman Road about a half mile west of the I-95 Bridge with what appeared to be a body in the roadway.

As I approached the covered object I found that it was a body and noticed obvious drag marks on the roadway, which led to the body. After speaking with Officers Mitchell and Wichtendahl, and Lieutenant Davis of the Criminal Investigations Bureau, it was determined that we were more than likely dealing with a homicide and not simply a traffic fatality.

It was decided that the Traffic Enforcement Section would film and record the evidence, following the trail of body fluids from the body at rest to the point of origin, which at this time had not been determined. PFC Mitchell would record the information via the video recorder, Officer Wichtendahl would document the evidence on paper, and I would take photographs using a 35mm camera and color film.

The process began at the body, which was covered with a yellow emergency blanket. The blanket was removed for a short period of time and I found that the body was lying face down, with the head facing west on Gorman Road. The body was fully in the westbound lane of travel and was wound in barbed wire three to four times. The body appeared to be that of a woman and the body was partially clothed. It looked as though the clothing had been ripped away as the body was being dragged along the roadway.

After photographing the body as it lay at the final rest, we began to follow the path of body fluids and pieces of tissue and clothing east along Gorman road. The path was very distinguishable because the fluids left a dark reddish mark on the roadway.

We followed the marks to a point in the roadway where, if you are traveling westbound, you have to make a hard right hand turn. It is at this turn where the body became entwined in the barbed wire. Along the eastbound roadside is a three-strand barbed wire fence that had been run into by the car, which dragged the body. The barbed wire on the body matched a missing lower strand of the fence line. A more in depth description will be detailed later," VonBriesen noted.

"After photographing the scene, we continued to walk east following the path. The path led over the bridge, which crossed over I-95 past the elementary school. The path continued on Gorman Road to Horsham Drive, around Horsham to the intersection of Knights Bridge Road where a woman's white shoe was found.

While we walked this path, both video film and color photographs were taken of the trail and any evidence discovered along the way. The evidence photographed included pieces of torn clothing, pieces of human tissue and hair, and a piece of the vehicle. The vehicle part was the driver's side B Pillar Seatbelt bracket cover. This was found at the point of rest of the body, and had the letters BMW molded into the underside of the bracket," VonBriesen said.

"Once the complete path had been walked and documented on film, we went back to the final resting place of the body, and found the Medical Examiner had arrived and begun his examination of the body. He had rolled the body over and it was obvious that this was the body of a woman who was, in my estimation, in her mid thirties. There was very little clothing left on the body, and what was left was torn and shredded. Both thighs had the entire layer of skin removed and the muscular tissue was showing along the length of both thighs. The right inner arm appeared to be in the same condition as the legs, with most of the skin removed from the shoulder to the elbow. Approximately the top third of the skull was missing, and appeared to have been ground off as the head was dragged along the roadway. Looking into the skull it seemed that an autopsy had already been performed because there was nothing inside but a small pool of blood. It was evident from the condition of the body, and from the trail left in the roadway, that the body had been dragged the entire distance from Horsham Drive and Knights Bridge Road to its final resting place on Gorman Road."

PFC VonBriesen went on. "I was assigned the task of determining whether the suspects ran into the barbed wire fence intentionally in an attempt to dislodge the body from the vehicle, or if the collision with the fence was accidental.

The examination of the roadway prior to and into the curve showed no skid marks from the suspect vehicle. The only marks on the roadway in the curve are the marks left from the body fluids of the victim.

The curve on Gorman Road comes at a location .2149 miles (1134.672 feet) west of the west side bridge expansion joint of the I-95 overpass. The curve is marked with a 20-Mile Per Hour warning sign below a yellow and black right turn arrow. This warning sign is placed .0689 miles (363.79 feet) before the curve. The curve itself is to the right and is almost a 90-degree angle turn. The sight distance to the curve as you travel west is .1523 miles (804.14 feet). The approach to the curve is straight with a slight down grade. Gorman Road is a two-lane road at this point with the lanes divided by a solid double yellow line, with white edge lines for the east and westbound lanes.

The suspect vehicle, traveling westbound on Gorman Road, dragging the victim from the left side headed into the curve. Forty to fifty feet into the curve the body fluid drag marks start to cross the double line and the body strikes a reflective roadside marker that is posted along the eastbound shoulder. The body continued along the eastbound shoulder and then crashed into one of the wooden posts, which support the barbed wire fence. While going past the iron gate in the fence, the body became intertwined in the barbed wire as the vehicle struck one of the wooden posts, knocking it down and dragging the barbed wire along the top and sides of the vehicle. The vehicle reentered the highway dragging the body now entwined in barbed wire, and continued west on Gorman Road for another 4 to 5 tenths of a mile before it was removed from the car.

Closer examination of the areas around the curve revealed that pieces of human tissue were left on the reflective roadside maker and west of the marker. Behind the fence to the east side of the gate, two larger pieces of tissue were discovered and some smaller pieces of tissue were found to the west side of the gate. Crime Scene Technicians recovered all sections of tissue for analysis.

Once again the roadway was checked for any signs that the car skidded into the fence and, as before, there were no skid marks on the roadway, which could be connected to this incident. The marks that were found were a set of Yaw marks on the east side road pavement. (A Yaw is the mark left on the road surface when a car is taking a turn too fast and the tire bounces off of the road surface.) Those marks showed that the vehicle, traveling west, went off of the east side of the roadway and into the fence. The path then leads back to the roadway and is directly in line with the body fluid marks left by the victim's body as she both left, and reentered the roadway.

The Yaw marks in the stone and dirt roadside indicate the path of a rolling, sliding tire and not one that is braking. The dirt and stones along this path were pushed to one side of the path, and that was to the left of the vehicle or to the outside of the direction of travel. Had these marks been skid marks, the stones and dirt would have been thrown from the path on both sides of the marks and the mark would look like a furrow in the dirt.

The Yaw Marks were photographed and measurements were taken of the chord and middle ordinate. The drag factor of the roadside was taken using a 30-pound drag sled. The results of the measurements are as follows: Chord of 27 feet, Middle ordinate of 9 (nine) inches, drag factor .58. With these measurements the exact speed of the vehicle in the Yaw was determined to be 32 miles per hour. The speed limit on the roadway is 30 miles per hour.

Due to the speed of the vehicle and the evidence found in the curve, it has been determined that the suspects drove the vehicle into the fence for the specific purpose of scraping the victim from the side of the car. The body hit the roadside marker prior to the vehicle going into the Yaw on the right roadside, and there is no evidence of excess speed in the curve. The position of the Yaw does not indicate that the driver lost control of the vehicle, but rather committed an intentional act, in an attempt to dislodge the body being dragged next to the car.

With the assistance of Officer Wills of the Baltimore City Police Department's Traffic Investigation Unit, and their reconstruction computer software and plotter printer, a scale diagram was completed using the measurements that were taken of the curve."

    Measurements were then taken by Officer Scott Wichtendahl to show the entire length of the scene and various points, including streets and evidence. Wichtendahl utilized Howard County Vascar Unit TV-5 for the purpose of obtaining the distances from the victim's residence to the final resting-place of the body.

Fatal Destiny

***

	Miles	Feet
House	0.0000	000.0
Stop Sign	0.0668	352'8"
Shoe	0.0722	381'2"
Hair	0.1348	711'8"
Body Scuff Start	0.1379	728'1"
Donan Castle	0.1570	828'11"
Gorman Road	0.3407	1798'10"
Stephens Road	0.9990	5274'8"
First piece of clothing	1.1868	6266'3"
I-95 Bridge (East Side)	1.2963	6844'5"
Pants	1.4030	7407'10"
Tissue Matter	1.4634	7726'9"
Curve in Roadway	1.5913	8402'1'
Body	1.8193	9605'10"
Total Length of Body Drag	1.6814	8877'9"
Total Length of Scene	1.7525	9253'2"

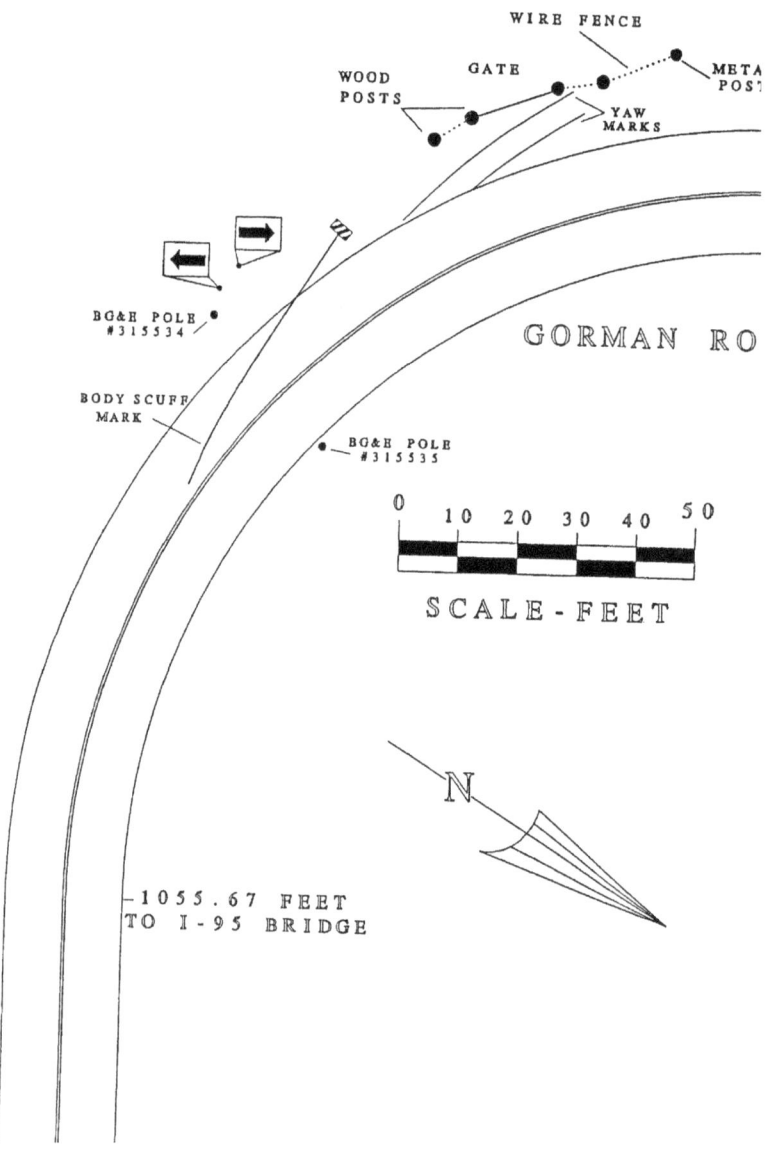

Five

As evidence in this incident pointed to homicide rather than a traffic fatality, a Command Post was established at the Forest Ridge Elementary School to direct operations. A Command Post is not employed as a matter of routine in homicide investigations, because a murder is usually confined within one location. Police are more often called to a home, apartment, store or a specific outside area where they can maintain security over the scene and keep evidence intact while they conduct their investigation. In this particular case however, the scene was spread over an area encompassing nearly two miles and evidence, valuable to investigators, was scattered over the entire route.

Detective First Class Thomas Martin responded to the school and would assume responsibility as the primary case investigator. Detective First Class Frank Dayhoff and Detective Lee Lachman would assist him during the course of the lengthy investigation.

One of their first tasks would be to identify, locate and interview the unusually large number of witnesses to this incident. Again, most homicide cases have few to no eyewitnesses to provide details to police. In this instance, there would be dozens.

While detectives were beginning to take statements from the witnesses, Solomon and Miller continued their flight to avoid apprehension. In an effort to rid themselves of evidence linking them to the viciously brutal crime, they began to throw items from the car. Fearing that his clothing had been spattered with Pam Basu's blood when he helped pull her body from the car, Miller took off his jogging pants and threw them from the car about three quarters of a mile beyond the body on Gorman Road. Next he removed his tee shirt and tossed it out along the roadside of Gorman Road near Martown Road.

Sometime just prior to 9:00 AM, Rhonda Pepper stopped behind a BMW at the intersection of Route 216 and U.S. Route 29. While waiting for the traffic signal to change she saw the driver's door open and a shoe fall, or was dropped to the road. She beeped her horn and called to the driver, "You dropped your shoe."

The driver, described by Pepper as a black male, smiled and waved her off. When the light changed he drove across Route 29 and continued traveling along Route 216. At this time the passenger began throwing paper napkins, penny rollers and plastic forks from the car.

"The vehicle began to swerve well on to the right shoulder as if the driver is reaching down," Pepper said. "Then he regained control."

Rhonda Pepper wrote down the tag number of WMN 492, and when she returned home she called and notified police of what she had seen.

Solomon and Miller continued to throw Pam Basu's personal belongings from the car. Her briefcase, a brown leather folder, purse, wallet and driver's license were thrown from the car at various locations over a radius of several miles. Her credit cards and case were removed from her purse and wallet before these items were thrown from the car.

For some time it seemed that they drove aimlessly about, searching for a way back to Washington, D. C. They drove along

Route 32 until they reached Eldersburg where they would attempt to destroy the last of the visible evidence that would draw attention to them. In what can only be described as a coldly calculated act, they drove into a car wash to flush away the blood of Pam Basu, which stained the driver's side of the car and the left rear wheel.

Randy Valonis, the car wash attendant, walked to the car and said, "What did you guys get into last night? That looks like blood."

"That ain't blood," Solomon, who was driving, said.

Valonis stated that he saw what looked like "chunks of vomit" on the side of the car when he started to scrub the driver's side and the left rear wheel.

While he was washing the left side of the car, the driver opened the door and called to him, "Get the wheel. Get the wheel."

After the car passed through the wash Valonis removed a damaged Russell BMW license plate frame and a black plastic air duct which was hanging from the vehicle. At about this same time Solomon asked Valonis if he could buy his watch. He said, "Yes," but the transaction ended.

"How do I get back to D. C.?" Solomon said after paying for the car wash.

"Go down Route 32 to 70," Valonis said.

Solomon then drove from the lot, turned south on Route 32 and began driving in the direction of I-70. As the car vanished from sight Valonis dropped the license plate frame and air duct into a trash can.

While Solomon and Miller were leaving the car wash in Eldersburg, Maryland State Police First Sergeant Scott Mergenthaler was stopping to check on the disabled Cadillac on I-95. He said, "The vehicle was occupied by a black male and a black female who were sleeping when I arrived. In questioning the subjects, I was informed that the car ran out of gas and that the other occupants had gone to get gas." After his conversation with them, Mergenthaler joined the search for the stolen BMW.

Trooper First Class Marc Price stopped by the Howard County District Court Commissioner's Office immediately after completing his testimony in a criminal case. While in the commissioner's office he monitored a radio broadcast detailing the theft of a BMW and murder of the owner during the theft. He noted that the stolen vehicle was last seen on Route 216 in the vicinity of Route 108, and was occupied by two black males. Price concluded his business at the commissioner's office and drove to the area of Route 108 to assist in the search for the car and suspects.

Trooper 8, a Maryland State Police Helicopter, being piloted by Corporal Scott Richardson, and with Trooper First Class Steven Proctor on board as assigned medic, responded to provide aerial assistance to ground units in the search for the stolen car.

Patrolling the roads around Routes 216 and 108 were Officer Donald Lundin of the Howard County Police as well as Sergeant A. T. Smith and Trooper First Class Russell Williams of the State Police. While they continued a roving patrol, Trooper First Class Marc Price saw the suspect vehicle traveling westbound on Route 108 just west of Ten Oaks Road. It was about 9:55 AM when he turned and gave chase.

When the driver of the BMW sped up to elude capture, Price radioed Sergeant Smith that the suspects were headed toward Route 216 and asked for assistance in stopping them.

Sergeant Smith, TFC Williams and Officer Lundin moved their police cruisers across the intersection of Routes 216 and 108 and established a stationary roadblock.

As they approached the intersection, TFC Price pulled out from behind the BMW, accelerated and moved his cruiser parallel to the driver's door of the fleeing car. At this time Price was looking to his right and directly at the driver of the BMW. Solomon hit the brakes of the BMW and stopped about a car length from the roadblock. He immediately threw the car in reverse and jammed the accelerator to the floor.

TFC Price quickly spun his cruiser around and took up pursuit of the fleeing car. The cars were faced front end to front end, with Price staring Solomon in the eyes as they drove.

The BMW careened backwards at a high rate of speed in an eastbound direction on Route 108, with County and State Police units in pursuit. The chase continued for almost a mile before Solomon lost control of the car, struck an embankment, went through a fence and into a field used to house dairy cattle.

When the car came to rest Solomon immediately jumped out and fled on foot, with Officer Lundin and Sergeant Smith giving chase. Miller also escaped from the car and attempted to flee, however his flight was hindered by heavy underbrush and TFCs Price and Williams apprehended him.

Solomon, who had the advantage of a considerable jump on his pursuers, was almost 200 yards ahead of them in the field and fleeing toward a residential area.

Trooper 8 was notified of the situation, and was overhead within 30 seconds. Officer Lundin waved to the crew, and pointed toward the corner of the field.

Trooper First Class Steven Proctor said, "A black male, approximately 20 years old, wearing black pants and a black tee shirt was running around a pond toward several houses and a wooded area. No other police officers were in close proximity, and it appeared that the suspect would disappear into the wooded area before he could be apprehended."

Corporal Richardson turned the helicopter in the direction of the fleeing suspect and put his aircraft just above and in front of Solomon in an effort to force him to stop. But he continued to run. Corporal Richardson set the helicopter down about 200 feet behind Solomon and TFC Proctor jumped from the aircraft and began pursuing him.

"I got out and ran after him," Proctor said. "As I caught up to him I shouted for him to stop several times, but he kept running. I drew my handgun and ordered him to stop and get down. He eventually stopped in the front yard of a large house somewhere off of Prestwick Drive. I ordered him to move his arms straight out to his sides. He refused and folded his arms under his chest. I moved his arms out to his sides, palms up, handcuffed him and searched him for weapons."

Only moments after being taken into custody and advised of his rights, and the crime for which he was arrested, Solomon said, "I don't know nothin' about it. I was out for a jog."

By now other County and State Police Officers were arriving on the scene of the apprehensions, among them Detectives Mark Miller, Kevin Burnett and Lee Lachman. Detective Burnett was instructed to take custody of Bernard Eric Miller and transport him to Howard County Police Headquarters. After being put into Burnett's car, Miller began a conversation by saying, "Excuse me, sir."

"Yes," Detective Burnett responded.

Miller blurted, "Rodney told me to get in the car. We were in a Cadillac that ran out of gas near the car pool and we needed a car. So Rodney went and got a car and told me to get in. There's two people in the Cadillac."

Detective Burnett radioed the Command Post and told them there was another car that had been abandoned because of running out of gas, and that it was possibly occupied by a black male and black female who were in some way connected to the incident.

Detective Lachman walked over to Burnett's car and Miller said to him, "Rodney grabbed the lady and took her car. He told me to get in."

Miller did not make any further comments and Lachman did not question him regarding his statements. However, he did take note of the clothing Miller was wearing: boxer shorts, high-topped athletic shoes and an athletic style jacket.

First Sergeant Scott Mergenthaler, who had monitored Detective Burnett's radio transmission, thought the Cadillac he had checked earlier was the vehicle in question. He returned to the area of the I-95 rest stop to speak with Tony Williams and LaShawn Smith.

Mergenthaler asked them for the identities of the persons who had left the vehicle to pick up gasoline. He was told that one was a black male named Rodney, who was dressed in black, and the other was a younger black male named "TJ" who was wearing a blue and orange sweat suit. As he continued to question them, they became evasive in their answers and balked at his attempts to obtain telephone numbers of anyone who would help them.

Now convinced that they were in some way involved with persons responsible for the carjacking and murder of Pam Basu, First Sergeant Mergenthaler transported them to Maryland State Police Barrack "A" in Jessup, Maryland for questioning by Howard County Police Investigators.

Sergeant Louis "Pete" D'Antuono of the Howard County Police met with First Sergeant Mergenthaler at Barrack "A" and was briefed on his encounter with Williams and Smith.

Sergeant D'Antuono conducted interviews with Tony Williams and LaShawn Smith after advising them of their Miranda Rights, and determining that they were capable of making a free and voluntary statement.

D'Antuono learned that Smith had been enrolled at the Woodstock Job Corps Center since July 28, 1992. She had been granted holiday leave for Labor Day Weekend and was due to return to the center on September 7th. However she had missed her bus and became stranded in D. C. At about 3:00 AM on September 8th, Rodney, Bernard Miller and Tony picked her up in a car she described as long and burgundy in color. She said they picked her up to drive her back to the Job Corps Center.

Although Rodney was given directions to the Job Corps Center, he didn't follow the instructions and they became lost.

After asking several people for directions to the Center, and still failing to locate it, Rodney decided to drive back to Washington, D. C. While traveling south on I-95, the car ran out of gas and they pulled to the side of the road. Rodney and "TJ" (Bernard Miller's nickname) left the car and said they were going for gas. Smith said that was the last time she saw them.

When asked to describe Rodney and "TJ", Smith said Rodney was a dark skinned black male, about 27 years of age and wearing a black Redskins tee shirt and black pants. She said "TJ" was a lighter skinned black male, about 16 or 17 years of age, who was wearing a blue or dark blue sweat suit. He was also wearing a white tee shirt with the initials "TJ" inscribed on the front.

When Sergeant D'Antuono interviewed Tony Williams he provided him with the same basic information given by LaShawn Smith.

Both parties were transported to Howard County Police Headquarters, where LaShawn Smith later gave a written statement to Detective First Class Thomas Martin. When questioned in depth by Martin she said that she had smoked some marijuana sometime on September 7th. She also told DFC Martin that Rodney and "TJ" had been smoking blunts (cigars emptied and filled with marijuana). She indicated that they had also been smoking Love Boat (marijuana laced with PCP).

Six

The driver of the BMW was turned over to Officers Robert Wagner and Ellsworth Jones for transport to Howard County Police Headquarters. When they arrived in the detention area Solomon was photographed, his clothing seized and placed in the drying room. His clothing had become covered in mud when he fell beside the pond while attempting to elude arrest.

Officer Jones gave him a white jump suit and escorted him to the Bull Pen (the holding cell) where he would be held until he was processed. Jones asked the suspect for his name in order to complete the detention log.

"Andre Johnson," he said.

Trooper First Class Marc Price met Officer Jones in the cellblock and identified the man in the Bull Pen as the driver of the BMW. "That's him," he said. "That's the driver."

When Officer Jones and TFC Price left the cellblock, Officer Susan Reider came in with a prisoner. The moment he saw Officer Reider, Solomon began blowing kisses to her and continued to do so at every opportunity. While she was fingerprinting her prisoner, Solomon pressed his lips against the glass observation window of the Bull Pen.

Fed up with his actions, Officer Reider taped a fingerprint card over the observation window and completed processing her prisoner without further interruptions.

Detective Lee Lachman removed Solomon from the Bull Pen and took him to an interview room. Lachman asked if the name Andre Johnson was his correct name. He informed him that he'd lied and that his real name was Harold Leroy Solomon of East Capitol Street, Washington, D. C. He also gave a partial Social Security number of 577-98.

"I advised Solomon of his Constitutional Rights per the Miranda decision via Howard County Police Department Form 1230," Lachman said. "Solomon said that he understood all of the rights explained to him, however he refused to sign or initial the form."

"I'm not signin' nothin'," Solomon said. "I wanna talk to a lawyer. I want a lawyer here when I answer questions."

Lachman immediately stopped his questioning of Solomon and returned him to the Bull Pen.

Detective Lachman ran a criminal history check on Harold Leroy Solomon and found there was a person by that name with identical date of birth. The first part of the Social Security number also matched the information given by Solomon. The criminal history check also revealed a FBI Identification Number of 810895X4 for this person.

Lachman asked Detective Mark Miller to fingerprint Solomon in order to have his prints compared with the classification for Harold Leroy Solomon. Miller took Solomon from the cell to fingerprint him, but he refused to have his prints rolled. When Miller told him that he'd stay in the cell until his fingerprints were obtained, Solomon agreed to be printed.

The inked impressions were then taken to Fingerprint Expert R. C. Bartley for comparison with the classification of Harold Leroy Solomon. After examining the prints Mr. Bartley determined that the person who was in custody was not Harold Leroy Solomon.

Lachman went to the cellblock and told Solomon that he had once again given a false name. Several minutes passed before Solomon finally told Lachman that his true identity was Rodney Eugene Solomon.

Lachman found there was a Rodney Eugene Solomon with a date of birth of 22 December 1965 and a FBI Identification Number of 215050DA8. When R. C. Bartley compared the inked prints with the fingerprint classification provided by Lachman he determined that the person under arrest was indeed Rodney Eugene Solomon.

Digging deeper into Rodney Eugene Solomon's background, it was discovered that he had prior arrests for robbery, theft, possession of contraband, distribution of cocaine, distribution of heroin and rioting while carrying a dangerous and deadly weapon. The latter charge was placed while he was serving a sentence for robbery in the Lorton Reformatory, Lorton, Virginia. For his part in the riot he received an additional three-year sentence. Furthermore, he had been afforded community supervision four times and on three occasions it was revoked. It was also learned that he had a revocation of parole in a District of Columbia robbery case. Court records would also show that Solomon had been arrested and charged in June 1991 with assault with intent to murder in a District Of Columbia Street shooting. Those charges were later dismissed.

The most shocking revelation and indeed the greatest anger provoking fact for Pam Basu's family, friends and neighbors was Solomon's release from jail only one week prior to this brutal crime.

Solomon had been jailed on May 4th in the District of Columbia on charges of possession with intent to distribute heroin. He was released on September 1st under the District's Bail Reform

Act of 1992. The act states, "A defendant can't be held in jail before trial solely because he can't afford the bail."

Associate D. C. Superior Court Judge Reggie Walton, who released Solomon said, "Under the circumstances it left no option but to release the individual as mandated by the law."

Mark Liedl, a spokesman for the United States Attorney's Office, said prosecutors had requested that Rodney Solomon be held without bail on the heroin charge during a hearing in the District of Columbia On May 11th because they felt he posed a danger to the community based on his prior record. "We requested that the defendant be held without bond. The court rejected our request," Mr. Liedl said. "It's within the judge's discretion."

Judge Walton placed certain conditions on the release of Solomon, including a 6:00 PM to 6:00 AM curfew. He also ordered that he verify his address with the D. C. Pretrial Services; attend a weekly drug program, report in person to Pretrial Services and refrain from crime.

Later, over 400 angry residents crowded into the cafeteria of the Forest Ridge Elementary School to meet with police officials, vent their feelings, and demand maximum penalties for Rodney Solomon and Bernard Miller.

When one person in attendance asked what the maximum penalty was for such a crime, Howard County Police Lieutenant Daniel Davis said, "There is a death penalty in the state."

The crowd erupted with applause.

There were, of course, the "What if" questions. "What if Rodney Solomon had remained in jail? What if Judge Walton had ignored the Bail Reform Act?"

Sadly, "What if" questions and theories would not give life back to Pam Basu, nor restore a devoted wife to Steve, and loving mother to Sarina.

Seven

As events of September 8th continued to unfold, Detective Kevin Burnett spoke with Detective Lachman, telling him that he'd provided Bernard Miller with food and a drink. After accepting the meal, Miller told Burnett that he wanted to talk with detectives about what had happened.

It was around noon when Lachman spoke with Miller and told him that police wanted to talk with him about the incident and listen to his side of the story. Miller said he wanted to talk with Lachman and tell him what happened.

Detective Lachman, with Detective Burnett present, advised Bernard Eric Miller of his Constitutional Rights and went over each line of the advice of rights form with him. Miller said that he understood his rights, wished to waive them and make a statement to police.

Detectives Lachman and Burnett did not tape Miller's initial account of the incident. However, the following is a verbatim transcript of the interview that took place at approximately 2:00 PM on September 8, 1992.

Lachman: Bernard, we're just going to go over everything step by step. Okay?
Miller: Yeah.

Lachman:	So, I need you to talk—to just kind of speak up a little bit, because, you know, don't whisper or anything like that. I need to be able to hear what you're saying. Okay"
Miller:	Yes.
Lachman:	So, describe for me what happened from the very beginning this morning. What time did you all first meet up with…
Miller:	I met 'em about one o'clock in the morning. At 58th and Blane.
Lachman:	Okay. You met Rodney?
Miller:	Yes.
Lachman:	And who else was with you?
Miller:	LaShawn and Little Tony.
Lachman:	Little Tony. Okay. And who had a car?
Miller:	Who had the car?
Lachman:	Uh huh.
Miller:	Rodney.
Lachman:	Rodney had a car. And what kind of car was it?
Miller:	A Cadillac.
Lachman:	Okay. And what color was it?
Miller:	Black and burgundy.
Lachman:	And where did he tell you he got the car?
Miller:	From Jonathan.
Lachman:	Jonathan who?
Miller:	The owner of the car.
Lachman:	Okay. In other words, what's his last name?
Miller:	Lovett.
Lachman:	And that's Lovett?
Miller:	Yeah.
Lachman:	And why'd he say he was borrowing the car?
Miller:	He was takin' LaShawn back to Job Corps.

Lachman:	Is LaShawn related to him or…
Miller:	No. A friend of Rodney.
Lachman:	Just a friend of Rodney?
Miller:	Yes.
Lachman:	What's Rodney's last name?
Miller:	Solomon.
Lachman:	Solomon?
Miller:	Yes.
Lachman:	And you met… Is your family kin to his family?
Miller:	Yes.
Lachman:	And related to his mother, Barbara?
Miller:	Yes.
Lachman:	And where does she live?
Miller:	5929 East Capitol Street.
Lachman:	Okay. And what does Rodney look like?
Miller:	He dark skin. About a hundred and—he's solid. He's solid.
Lachman:	Okay. How old is he? About?
Miller:	About 26.
Lachman:	Okay. I showed you a picture of someone before and you identified that person as Rodney.
Miller:	Yes.
Lachman:	Okay. So, after you all got together and you're in the car, where were you going?
Miller:	Take LaShawn back to Baltimore—the bus station.
Lachman:	Okay. And she's going where?
Miller:	Um, Job Corps.
Lachman:	Job Corps?
Miller:	The bus had already left. So we took her to Baltimore. We was takin' her, uh, to the Job Corps Center.

Lachman:	You were going to take her out to Job Corps?
Miller:	Yes.
Lachman:	And what happened?
Miller:	The car ran out of gas. So we pulled over at a little rest area.
Lachman:	And what was at the rest area?
Miller:	A vending machine and a telephone booth.
Lachman:	Was there trucks there?
Miller:	Yes.
Lachman:	Okay. Was that on a main road? Do you know what route or road you were on?
Miller:	I ain't remember.
Lachman:	Was it a big road?
Miller:	Yes.
Lachman:	Was it like an Interstate Highway?
Miller:	Yes.
Lachman:	Okay. So, what happened while you all were there?
Miller:	The car ran out of gas.
Lachman:	Okay.
Miller:	We went to the vending machines to use the phone.
Lachman:	Okay.
Miller:	And Rodney got out of the car. Left LaShawn and Tony in the car.
Lachman:	Uh huh.
Miller:	Rodney told me we was going to get a ride.
Lachman:	Uh huh.
Miller:	He had first seen a car where some people were standing at. Where some townhouses was at.
Lachman:	Yes.
Miller:	And he saw a lady.

Lachman:	Now the first person you saw…
Miller:	First we saw a lady. We asked her if we could use the phone.
Lachman:	Uh huh.
Miller:	She say—um she was goin' on—ask the lady up the street if you can use the phone. So, we walked up there.
Lachman:	When you asked her to use the phone… What did she look like? The first lady you asked to use the phone?
Miller:	She was short and red. Short and—she was fat. She had a baby in a Caravan—a burgundy Caravan.
Lachman:	Okay. And what color hair did she have?
Miller:	Blonde.
Lachman:	The first lady you saw.
Miller:	Yes.
Lachman:	And the Caravan was what color?
Miller:	Burgundy.
Lachman:	All right. So, so you asked her to use the phone and she said…
Miller:	No.
Lachman:	No? Okay, then what happened?
Miller:	So Rodney—um—walked around on—around the house, right.
Lachman:	Okay.
Miller:	The lady say—um—she say, she say she was gonna call for help. She say, 'I can identify you.' Rodney say—uh, we ain't tryin' to cause no problem with you. We just run out of gas. We want to use the phone. She said no. So we left.
Lachman:	Uh huh.

Miller:	Walked away—went down the street to some townhouses. We saw a champagne—burgundy—um, brown BMW.
Lachman:	Yes.
Miller:	Rodney grabbed the lady.
Lachman:	Okay.
Miller:	Choked her. Slammed the car door and pulled off with the lady. And drove off with the lady in the car.
Lachman:	Where were you when Rodney grabbed and choked the lady?
Miller:	I was on the other side of the house. He pulled around saying get in.
Lachman:	Uh huh.
Miller:	I got in the car. Then I started smelling this little odor.
Lachman:	Uh huh.
Miller:	Then he saw—we stopped the car and the lady was hangin'—she was layin' on the ground with the seat belt hooked to her left arm.
Lachman:	Okay.
Miller:	Rodney yanked her arm off and then we pulled off and the baby was in the back seat crying behind me.
Lachman:	Okay.
Miller:	He took the baby out the back seat, put the baby on the ground. He pulled off, drove up the street, drove a ways and went to the gas station.
Lachman:	Okay.
Miller:	Put some gas in the car then went to a car wash.
Lachman:	Okay.

Miller:	Went to the car wash. Then that's when we left from the car wash and went to another gas station to ask direction. And the man said um, police are around askin' for a brown BMW. So I said, Rodney he callin' the police. So Rodney say, get in the car, get in the car. So we pulled off from the gas station. I say he callin' the police. Then the roadblock was up the street. We backed up. Rodney was backin'. He was swervin' real fast. Fast. Fast. Goin' real fast backwards.
Lachman:	Uh huh.
Miller:	Then we went up to a barn. That's when the police pulled out their guns and put it on the ground. Rodney and Rodney say, run, run, run. Run, run, youngin', run he said. He was tellin' me he was goin' to see me straight. He said don't say nothin' about this. When we get home you—we see you straight. I had got locked up. They asked me questions.
Lachman:	Now, when you were talking to me earlier, you said that you saw the lady with the BMW...
Miller:	Yeah.
Lachman:	Okay.
Miller:	I was standin' on the other side of the house.
Lachman:	Right.
Miller:	Rodney say he was gonna come around. He said I'm a see if I can get the car from the lady.
Lachman:	Now...
Miller:	I seen, I seen, I seen him push the lady.

Lachman:	Now, when he said that... I mean, obviously she wasn't going to give him the car keys.
Miller:	Yeah. She say, help, help.
Lachman:	I mean like that. When he said he was going to go get the car from the lady, he meant he was gonna take the car from the lady, right?
Miller:	Yeah. Yeah.
Lachman:	I mean he was going to steal the car from the lady, right?
Miller:	Yes.
Lachman:	All right. She obviously wasn't going to lend it to him?
Miller:	Yeah. Right.
Lachman:	So he told you that before he went over to her?
Miller:	Yeah.
Lachman:	That he was going to take the car from her?
Miller:	Yes. I was standin' around the other side waitin' for him.
Lachman:	Do you remember exactly what he said?
Miller:	He said wait right here. He say, I'm gonna, he say I'm gonna take the car from her.
Lachman:	Okay.
Miller:	I was waitin' for him. Next thing I know he pulled around and said get in.
Lachman:	Now, from where you were standing you saw what happened, right?
Miller:	Yeah.
Lachman:	Okay, and what happened?
Miller:	Next thing you know...
Lachman:	In other words, when he first went up to the lady, where was she?

Miller:	She was standin', she was standin' on the outside of the car.
Lachman:	Okay, was the door open?
Miller:	And then… Yeah. He tried to—he snatched her out. She was still had the seatbelt on.
Lachman:	She was in the car?
Miller:	Yeah.
Lachman:	Okay.
Miller:	He pulled off with her in there.
Lachman:	Okay. So, when he first went up there he pulled her out of the car?
Miller:	Yep.
Lachman:	Okay.
Miller:	But she still had the seat belt on.
Lachman:	Okay. And the seatbelt was…
Miller:	He drove off and yanked her.
Lachman:	Okay. Now, when he pulled her out of the car, you said he was chokin' her?
Miller:	Yeah.
Lachman:	And at that point, where were you?
Miller:	I was waitin' for him to come around the corner.
Lachman:	You were waiting for him around the corner?
Miller:	Uh huh.
Lachman:	All right. Now, when he came around the corner, what happened?
Miller:	Then he came around the corner. I got in the car.
Lachman:	When you got in the car, you got in on the passenger's side?
Miller:	I got—climbed into the driver's side on to the other side.

Lachman:	You climbed through the driver's side?
Miller:	Me and him was tanglin' up with each other. I saw the lady.
Lachman:	So, in other words when you got in the car you got in through the driver's side rear door?
Miller:	Yeah. Yeah.
Lachman:	And you and the lady were tangling up with each other?
Miller:	Uh huh.
Lachman:	Okay. Now, describe that for me. Like...
Miller:	She was laying down and I seen her butt hangin' out and her left arm and he just pulled off with me and her and kept sayin' just calm down. I sayin' I ain't. I thought she was, thought she was left out. I didn't know she was still hooked on to the car, right.
Lachman:	Yes.
Miller:	He snatched her off.
Lachman:	In other words, when he pulled off after you got tangled up with her and got in the car, you thought that she had fallen off?
Miller:	Yeah.
Lachman:	So, when you first got in the car, you got in through the driver's side in the rear door, right?
Miller:	Yes.
Lachman:	Okay. And was the baby in the back seat with you?
Miller:	Yes.
Lachman:	And when you went to get in the car, she was laying on the ground and you got tangled up with her. How?

Miller:	She was hooked up. She was hooked on the door.
Lachman:	Right, she was hooked on the door.
Miller:	Yeah.
Lachman:	So, you kind of had to get her out of the way to get in?
Miller:	Yeah. Yeah.
Lachman:	Was she conscious?
Miller:	She ain't sayin'—she wasn't sayin' nothin'.
Lachman:	Was she like, you know…
Miller:	She was unconscious. She wasn't sayin' nothin'. She was just…
Lachman:	Just layin' there?
Miller:	Yeah, with her face down. Hooked up to—uh, her butt was hangin' in the air.
Lachman:	So, then you got in the car. And did you crawl into the front passenger's seat?
Miller:	Yeah.
Lachman:	Then what happened?
Miller:	Then Rodney pulled off with me in the car.
Lachman:	Okay…
Miller:	He said, don't say nothin'. He said I'm gonna see you straight. Then we started throwin' her items out the car.
Lachman:	Uh huh.
Miller:	We had the Most Card, the Crestar and there was Hecht's card.
Lachman:	And you took that out of what?
Miller:	Um, a little wallet. It was—it was a Fendi bag or somethin'.
Lachman:	Okay, some type of bag. What color was the bag?
Miller:	Like brown and white.
Lachman:	So the credit cards came out of the wallet?

Miller:	Um, and it was a SAAB bag in the back.
Lachman:	Who got the cards out of the wallet?
Miller:	I did.
Lachman:	And…
Miller:	Rodney took 'em from me and put 'em over the…
Lachman:	Visor?
Miller:	Yeah. He took 'em. He put…
Lachman:	Sun visor?
Miller:	No. Right over the—um; flip thing that you look in the mirror.
Lachman:	Yeah. It's called a sun visor. Sun visor.
Miller:	Yeah, sun visor.
Lachman:	So there's a SAAB bag in the back?
Miller:	Um.
Lachman:	What color is that?
Miller:	Black and red.
Lachman:	Okay. And did you look through that also.
Miller:	Uh huh.
Lachman:	And after you looked through that, what did you do with it?
Miller:	I threw it out the window.
Lachman:	Now, did you take anything out of the SAAB bag?
Miller:	Yeah.
Lachman:	What:
Miller:	There was some papers in there.
Lachman:	Papers? What kind of papers?
Miller:	Man, they was a pink piece of paper, like receipts and stuff.
Lachman:	Okay. And did you throw that out of the window?
Miller:	Mmmmm.

Lachman:	Did you throw the pocketbook out the window?
Miller:	And they was some white shoes in—there was some white shoes in the back of the car and Rodney threw the shoes out at the light.
Lachman:	Uh huh.
Miller:	And there was a car bumpin' the horn sayin' your shoes, you dropped your shoes. Rodney say we don't need the shoes and the lady started laughin'.
Lachman:	Yes.
Miller:	He pulled through the light.
Lachman:	Yes.
Miller:	That's when the roadblock was up there. He backed up real fast. He drove backwards.
Lachman:	Uh huh.
Miller:	Then he drove into the barn. Boom. The police say don't move.
Lachman:	Uh huh.
Miller:	I stopped. My chin was bleedin'. The police slammed me up against the car and said don't move. They handcuffed me. I was on my knees and I started talkin' to you.
Lachman:	Now, at what point after you got in the car through the driver's side door, after he picked you up and you got tangled up with the woman and then got untangled, you crawled into the passenger's seat and took off.
Miller:	Yeah.
Lachman:	How long… Was it a short distance between when you stopped and…
Miller:	You know what?
Lachman:	What?

Miller:	I was drivin' the car.
Lachman:	You were driving? At what point?
Miller:	Me and Rodney, we was drivin'. He was sittin' on—I think he was sittin'… The lady was hooked up.
Lachman:	Uh huh.
Miller:	And he was standin' on top of me sayin' move over. He was tryin' to push me over to the other side. But I'm sayin' I was still tryin' to drive at the same time.
Lachman:	Yes.
Miller:	But I was nervous.
Lachman:	Mmmmm.
Miller:	Then he pushed me over.
Lachman:	Uh huh.
Miller:	Then that's when I saw the lady hangin' and then we stopped the car. He snatched the lady off and the baby was cryin' in the back seat.
Lachman:	Okay, let's go over that again. When you first went up to the car and when you all first drove off, who was driving?
Miller:	Me.
Lachman:	You were driving. Okay, where was Rodney?
Miller:	He was pushin' the lady out the car.
Lachman:	He was pushin' the lady out of the car?
Miller:	Yeah. I started the car up.
Lachman:	You started it up?
Miller:	And then that's when he just said move over and he just started drivin'.
Lachman:	Rodney went up and grabbed the lady out of the car? Now, who went up and grabbed the woman out of the car?

Miller:	Rodney.
Lachman:	Rodney. And she had her seatbelt on?
Miller:	Yeah.
Lachman:	And while he was wrestling with the woman, you got in the car and started it up?
Miller:	Mmmm.
Lachman:	Is that right?
Miller:	But I ain't never press on the gas though.
Lachman:	So you…
Miller:	So he pushed me over and then he started drivin'.
Lachman:	Okay.
Miller:	So he dragged the lady.
Lachman:	So in other words, when Rodney first went up to the car and you went up to the car, did he have to open the door to get the woman out?
Miller:	The lady was still—she was hooked and she had her seatbelt on.
Lachman:	In other words, when you first went up to the car, was her door closed or opened?
Miller:	Was it closed or opened?
Lachman:	Yeah. When you and Rodney first went up to the car?
Miller:	It was open.
Lachman:	Okay, her door was open.
Miller:	And he slammed her. He slammed the door closed.
Lachman:	Okay.
Miller:	Easy, I was…
Lachman:	Let me see if I understand this, okay? So you all went up to the car. Rodney grabbed her out of the car, right? Is that right?
Miller:	Yes.

Lachman:	And when he grabbed her out of the car, you got in the driver's seat?
Miller:	Mmmm.
Lachman:	And then you started the car up?
Miller:	But I ain't never pull off.
Lachman:	You didn't pull off?
Miller:	No.
Lachman:	Then what happened?
Miller:	Then he pushed me over and pulled off with the lady still—she was still hung up in there.
Lachman:	Could you see that?
Miller:	Yeah.
Lachman:	You could see her hung up in there?
Miller:	Yeah. And I just started smellin'…
Lachman:	Uh huh.
Miller:	And I see her arm hooked on the seatbelt. He stopped the car.
Lachman:	Okay.
Miller:	He snatched the lady. He let her go. She was just layin' right there.
Lachman:	Okay.
Miller:	He pulled off. The baby was in the backseat cryin.' Then he took—he ran on the other side and pushed the baby in the grass. He set the baby on the grass and he started—he drove off.
Lachman:	Okay.
Miller:	Left the baby right there and he rolled up, and the baby was gone.
Lachman:	Now, when he took the seatbelt off of her arm, how did he have to get it off her arm?
Miller:	He snatched it off.
Lachman:	Like, pulled it real hard?
Miller:	He yanked it off.

Lachman:	Yanked it off?
Miller:	And her butt was just hangin' there like raw meat.
Lachman:	Like raw meat?
Miller:	Yeah. And you could smell her flesh.
Lachman:	You could smell her flesh. And then after you drove off, that's when you went through the purse?
Miller:	Mmmm.
Lachman:	And you got the credit cards out and you threw the purse out the window?
Miller:	I was throwin' the stuff out the window while Rodney was drivin' the car.
Lachman:	Okay. And the black bag from the back—the SAAB bag, you took some papers out of that?
Miller:	Yeah.
Lachman:	You threw the bag out the window. What else was in the bag?
Miller:	It was little like books and uh, it was a pencil.
Lachman:	Okay. And then…
Miller:	And some shoes in the back.
Lachman:	There were some shoes? And what color were they?
Miller:	White. And Rodney threw the shoes at that light…
Lachman:	The traffic light?
Miller:	And the lady beeped the horn sayin' you threw—you left your shoes.
Lachman:	Uh huh.
Miller:	He said I don't need 'em and the lady started laughin'.
Lachman:	Uh huh.

Miller:	And he pulled off.
Lachman:	After you pulled off from the light, where did you go next?
Miller:	He was drivin' to—he said he was tryin' to find the main highway.
Lachman:	Okay.
Miller:	That's when we pulled to the car wash. We got the car washed.
Lachman:	You got the car washed.
Miller:	Then we went to the gas station and the man say the police was just now lookin'.
Lachman:	Now, let's get back to the car wash. You went to the car wash for what purpose?
Miller:	To get the blood off the car.
Lachman:	To get the blood off. Okay.
Miller:	Yep.
Lachman:	And there was a guy at the car wash when you first went there?
Miller:	Uh huh.
Lachman:	And did the guy ask you what the blood was doing there or anything? Or did…
Miller:	No. He said uh, he say who crashed the car? But we crashed the car when Rodney was tryin' to get me out the seat.
Lachman:	Right.
Miller:	But I ain't never pull off though. It just (here Miller mumbles making car like noises) and it just skirt and then boom. We hit some…
Lachman:	You crashed the car?
Miller:	Yeah.
Lachman:	Into what?

Miller:	All I know we had hit somethin'. You know what I'm sayin'? We was just now pulling off though.
Lachman:	Oh, you were just pulling off?
Miller:	Yep.
Lachman:	Okay. And he was pushing you out of the driver's seat?
Miller:	Yeah. He was pushin' me out…
Lachman:	When you hit something?
Miller:	Yeah.
Lachman:	Now, when you went to the gas station… Not the gas station, the car wash. Did the guy at the car wash say anything to you about what was on the car or anything?
Miller:	No. He said uh, how you um, how did you wreck the car? He said the antenna was bent.
Lachman:	Okay.
Miller:	He said the antenna bent. Rodney tried to bend the antenna back while the dude was washin' the car.
Lachman:	And you said the guy had a scrub brush and a hose and he was washing the blood off?
Miller:	Mmmm.
Lachman:	Okay. What'd the guy look like? White guy?
Miller:	Yep, he was white. Tall and skinny.
Lachman:	About how old?
Miller:	He had to like thirty-five, thirty-six.
Lachman:	Thirty-five, thirty-six. And you said something about Rodney. What was he trying to do?
Miller:	Buy his watch.
Lachman:	Buy his watch. What was Rodney saying?

Miller:	Uh, hey, man, do you want to sell your watch? He said that's—he said, yeah, I like the watch. He said you want to buy this watch? He said yeah. Then... But Rodney never did buy the watch from him. Then we rode up to the other gas station.
Lachman:	So, you got it all washed off. Then what?
Miller:	We left from the car wash. We was drivin' some ways tryin' to find the main highway.
Lachman:	Okay.
Miller:	Then we pulled up to a gas station.
Lachman:	Yes.
Miller:	Then that's when the dude say, uh the police are in askin for a brown BMW. I said Rodney he callin' the police, he callin' the police. Rodney say, get in, get in, get in. We pulled off from the gas station.
Lachman:	Yes.
Miller:	Then uh, that's when we seen the roadblock up there. It was a police car behind us though followin' us. And Rodney just started backin' backwards real fast. Backed all the way up the street. That's when we went up to the little barn. I jumped on the front of the—I jumped from the other side of the hood. Police was standin' holdin' the gun sayin' don't move, don't move. That was that.
Lachman:	And then Rodney took off running?
Miller:	And Rodney took off running'.
Lachman:	Okay. If there's anything else we're... So, you don't know what happened to the other two people who were with you earlier?

Miller:	They was still in the car. They was still in the Cadillac at the rest area.
Lachman:	They were still in the Cadillac. And where was the Cadillac?
Miller:	It was in the middle of the highway.
Lachman:	When you originally left that area and went down into the town-house complex, the first time you knew that the car was going to be stolen was when Rodney told you, 'I'm gonna take that woman's car.'
Miller:	Uh huh.
Lachman:	And that's when the two of you went up to the car and he grabbed the woman and you got into the driver's seat and started it up?
Miller:	No. We was talkin' to another lady first.
Lachman:	Yeah, yeah. First you talked to that lady. But we're talking about the actual scenario of what happened with the BMW.
Miller:	Yeah.
Lachman:	Was that correct?
Miller:	Yes.
Lachman:	Okay. Before you stole the car, what did the lady look like at the BMW? What did she look like? Describe her.
Miller:	She was like a short Indian lady. She had long hair and it looked like she was red.
Lachman:	She was a white person, but she had a red complexion?
Miller:	Mmmm.
Lachman:	Is that right? She looked like she was Indian?
Miller:	Mmmm.
Lachman:	What did the baby look like?
Miller:	It was white. Like a white Chinese baby.

Lachman:	And the car that the baby was in was the same car that you were in when you wrecked and the police caught you?
Miller:	Mmmm.
Lachman:	All right, I think that about covers it. Okay.

Detective Lachman ended the taped interview with Bernard Eric Miller at about 2:25 PM. It was noted by Lachman during the initial interview, which was not taped, that Miller, when he said, "Flesh stinks" canted his head slightly back, flared his nostrils and breathed in deeply, describing the smell afterwards.

When he made the statement of seeing her buttocks and the raw meat of her flesh hanging off her body, he again canted his head back slightly, flared his nostrils and breathed in deeply saying, "It smelled bad. Her clothes were just ripped off her body."

After his taped statement, Miller was taken back to his cell to be held for processing and transport to the District Court Commissioner's Office for a bond review hearing.

Eight

The fact that Rodney Eugene Solomon and Bernard Eric Miller were arrested while attempting to flee from Pam Basu's stolen car does not necessarily guarantee a conviction in a court of law for the crime of murder. A defense attorney needs only to create a shadow of doubt in the minds of the jurors in order to have a verdict of Not Guilty handed down. It is therefore imperative that police and prosecutors present corroborating physical evidence with eyewitness testimony.

Eyewitness testimony may often times be marked with the emotion of the person presenting his or her statements to members of the jury. Physical evidence, such as fingerprints or bloodstain analysis "testifies" without emotion. Physical evidence presents scientific facts by which jurors may determine innocence as well as guilt of a defendant. It cannot speculate or offer an opinion as to the guilt or innocence of the accused party or parties.

It takes a very special person to work in the field where evidence is gathered, packaged, marked and analyzed. It is not a job for those in a hurry as the collection; preservation and identification of crime scene evidence often require painstaking efforts. Nor is it a field for the faint of heart because many bloody and horrifying sights will pass before those choosing to toil in law enforcement's realm of physical evidence.

Crime Scene Technicians Lisa Smith and Doug Read of the Howard County Police Department were called in this case to collect and process evidence. September 8th would be the first of many long, tedious days they would spend working to preserve and identify physical evidence.

CST Lisa Smith stopped first at the Cadillac on southbound Interstate 95 where Trooper Kevin Ringgold was standing by with the car. She processed the car for finger-prints and developed prints at several locations on the vehicle including the interior rearview mirror, front and rear passenger's side windows, driver's and passenger's side outside rearview mirrors and the driver's outside door handle. She also collected a number of items from the car and held them for processing. Photographs were then take to show the exact location of the car on I-95.

CST Smith then proceeded to the northbound I-95 rest stop where Police Officer William Block was maintaining custody of Grace Lagana's Chrysler Labaron. Smith was able to develop prints on the outside driver's door, the rear fender on the passenger's side and on the inside passenger's window. She took photographs of Lagana's car to show its exact location in the rest stop and proceeded to her next assignment on Gorman Road.

After arriving on Gorman Road she began collecting and packaging evidence listed in her report as follows:

4941-19	Skull/tissue fragment recovered from bent pole
4941-20	Tissue fragment recovered from bent pole
4941-21	Tissue fragment recovered from grass behind wire fence
4941-22	Tissue fragment from the wire fence
4941-23	Tissue fragment from wooden stake

CST Doug Read met Police Officer Brian Fuller on Gorman Road approximately one-quarter mile east of

Murray Hill Road. There he photographed and collected one pair of Navy Blue jogging pants, which had been found lying in the west-bound lane of Gorman Road. Read's report states, "The pants were wet to the touch, with a pink color noticed about the white trim."

CST Read continued collecting and packaging evidence along the entire route of the crime scene as follows:

The B Pillar seatbelt bracket cover for the left side of a BMW

A ladies left shoe (Impo Brand)

A small black rubber wheel

Bloodstained ladies panties

A pair of bloodstained pink slacks

He also noted what he described as, "A distinct drag mark on the surface of the roadway. This drag mark was continuous in a westerly direction for approximately 1-¾ miles, ending with the body of Mrs. Basu. The drag mark consisted of debris that appeared to contain minute particles of bone, blood and skin tissue."

CST Read also went to the Eldersburg Car Wash where he collected the plastic air duct vent and registration plate bracket from the BMW.

As telephone calls reporting the sighting of Mrs. Basu's personal belongings began coming in, Detective David Trapani and Officer Les Stickles were dispatched to retrieve them. The below listed items were recovered and turned over to Crime Scene Technicians for processing:

A brown leather folder

One briefcase

A white shoe

Miscellaneous papers

While physical evidence was being collected, efforts continued to locate and interview witnesses to the crime. While Detective First Class Frank Dayhoff interviewed the victim's husband, Steve Basu, Officer Brook Donovan canvassed the neighborhood in an effort to locate anyone who could provide information pertinent to the investigation.

Officer Donovan eventually spoke with Julie Panzeri who told him she saw Steve Basu videotaping Pam and Sarina as they left the house that morning. She also told him she saw two black males walking by, and one of them was looking at Pam and her car. After providing Donovan with a description of the two black males, he relayed the information to DFC Frank Dayhoff.

Dayhoff then spoke with Steve Basu and asked about the videotape. Mr. Basu gave the tape to Dayhoff who then viewed it privately at the house. Near the end of the tape two black males enter the screen walking from left to right. One is wearing black pants, has a black shirt draped around his neck and shoulders and is walking in the street. A thinner, younger male who is walking on the sidewalk follows him. As the scene continues to unfold the first man turns his head and glances over his left shoulder toward the man behind him. While his right arm swings by his side his hand turns sharply to the right with his fingers pointing to the BMW. A few seconds later, the men vanish from the screen.

DFC Dayhoff took the tape to police headquarters and, after reviewing it there, learned that the two men on the tape are Rodney Eugene Solomon and Bernard Eric Miller who have been arrested for the crime.

Although the foundation for the case is beginning to take shape, the difficult task of completing it is far from over.

Nine

At about 4:35 PM Detective Lachman was making a routine check of the suspect, Rodney Solomon, when Solomon began a conversation with him. At that time Solomon said he'd changed his mind and wanted to make a statement about the incident. He was taken from the Bullpen and escorted to an interview room where Detective First Class Thomas Martin joined them. The following is a transcript of the taped interview with Solomon.

Lachman:	Okay, it's September 8, 1992. It's 4:39 PM and I'm here with Rodney Solomon.
Solomon:	Yeah.
Lachman:	He's a Black male and his birth date 12-22-65. Rodney, obviously this is the second time today that I've been in an interview room with you, right? Detective Tom Martin's also present this time, okay? The first time you were with me you indicated immediately that you wanted to talk to a lawyer.
Solomon:	Yeah.

Lachman:	And you wanted to have him with you and present during questioning.
Solomon:	Yeah. 'Cause I know I'm not guilty. Yeah, I know I ain't do anything. Yeah. Okay.
Lachman:	Okay.
Solomon:	All right.
Lachman:	Now, when I was downstairs earlier—just a few minutes ago, I came and asked you if you'd been processed, is that right?
Solomon:	Yeah.
Lachman:	All right, I came in and asked if you'd been processed, right?
Solomon:	Right.
Lachman:	Okay.
Solomon:	I can say exactly what happened. I can tell you right…
Lachman:	Okay, okay, wait a minute. Wait a minute. We've got to go over some things now. All right, just to let you know Mr. Solomon just got a glass of water. He asked for a glass of water and they are getting him one. Is that correct?
Solomon:	Why you all got to tell all that? So that the judge is going to hear all this or somethin'? And the prosecutor's going to hear all this?
Lachman:	Well, I just have to explain things, okay? 'Cause obviously, you know, stopping in the middle of the sentence and all of a sudden there's nothing. I just want to…
Solomon:	Yeah, I got some water. I got some water, all right? Now…
Lachman:	So, a few minutes ago I came into the cell area and asked you if you'd been processed. Is that right?

Solomon:	Yeah.
Lachman:	Okay. And at that point you initiated a conversation with me, is that right?
Solomon:	Yeah.
Lachman:	And basically you're asking me what was going on with the other person involved in this?
Solomon:	Right.
Lachman:	Okay. And during that conversation you told me you wanted to talk with me, is that right?
Solomon:	Right.
Lachman:	Okay, I didn't come to you and say, Mr. Solomon I want you to make a statement. Or Mr. Solomon, I want to question you again. Or Mr. Solomon, I want you to come upstairs and say something. Is that right?
Solomon:	You got any donuts? Yeah?
Martin:	Donuts?
Solomon:	Yeah.
Lachman:	Donuts? We don't have any donuts. Mr. Solomon is getting a second glass of water. So, it's perfectly clear that I didn't come to you and ask you to answer questions. Is that right?
Solomon:	Yeah.
Lachman:	Okay. And you came to me and said you wanted to talk to me.
Solomon:	Mmmm.
Lachman:	Is that right?
Solomon:	Yeah.
Lachman:	And you said that you wanted to make a statement in your own words, is that right?
Solomon:	Yeah.

Lachman:	And you're here now. Now, before we can make the statement, obviously I'm gonna have to read this Miranda form to you again.
Solomon:	Let me see it.
Lachman:	Okay. I want to go over it with you here.
Solomon:	When everything happened I was around. But I—what I, but I didn't do it. Yeah, he did it. Is you all goin' to move me to the county jail or somethin'? I gonna get me outta here. I'm gonna get you some legit information. The truth, right and you'll move me outta here?
Martin:	(Inaudible) that's what we want is the truth. We're going to transport you when we get all the paperwork done.
Solomon:	Okay. What—what's up with Shawn?
Martin:	LaShawn?
Solomon:	Yeah.
Martin:	She's going to the Job Corps. I just talked to her.
Solomon:	When?
Martin:	As we speak.
Solomon:	Ya'll gonna take her?
Martin:	Uh huh.
Solomon:	Okay that's cool. That's cool. 'Cause she had nothin' to do with this. That's cool. (Inaudible) lie.
Lachman:	Okay. Right now you need to go over your sobriety. Are you currently under the influence of any drugs or alcohol?
Solomon:	No. I told that to you. I'm on medication. I'm all right though.
Lachman:	Okay.
Solomon:	I don't use drugs.

Lachman:	Now, have you been drinking any booze or alcohol? Or, have you taken any illicit drugs, anything illegal?
Solomon:	Nope.
Lachman:	So, you're sober, right? You're sober?
Solomon:	Yeah, I'm sober. I know what happened. I can tell you like it happened.
Lachman:	Okay, wait a minute.
Solomon:	Yeah.
Lachman:	Now, how far did you go in school?
Solomon:	Twelfth grade. Yeah.
Lachman:	Twelfth grade. You graduated?
Solomon:	Yeah.
Lachman:	High school?
Solomon:	Yeah.
Lachman:	Which high school did you graduate from?
Solomon:	Dunbar.
Lachman:	Dunbar? In Baltimore City?
Solomon:	No, D. C.
Lachman:	Dunbar High School in D. C.?
Solomon:	Went to college three years at U.D.C.
Lachman:	Three years at where?
Solomon:	Two. Two years at U.D.C. College. Yeah. Yeah.
Lachman:	Two years at what?
Solomon:	U.D.C. College.
Lachman:	University of D. C.?
Solomon:	Yeah. I probably can help you out on some other things. Yeah.
Lachman:	What did you major in at…
Solomon:	Business Management.
Lachman:	Business Management?
Solomon:	Business Management. Yeah.

Lachman:	Business Management. Obviously you read and write the English Language.
Solomon:	Yeah.
Lachman:	So, you currently take medication for what?
Solomon:	For uh, my mental stress. I got a lawsuit. That's right. I got a lawsuit and that's all.
Lachman:	You're taking medication for mental stress?
Solomon:	Yeah.
Lachman:	Did you take any today?
Solomon:	Yesterday. Today I've been here all day. How can I take anything?
Lachman:	Well, I don't know if you took some earlier this morning or what. What does the medication do to you?
Solomon:	It's nothing. It's just like a sedaform. Makes you sleep that's all.
Lachman:	A sedative?
Solomon:	Yeah. Yeah, that's all. Yeah.
Lachman:	Okay. And you take one a day?
Solomon:	Yeah.
Lachman:	What, before you go to sleep?
Solomon:	Yeah.
Lachman:	And it helps you sleep?
Solomon:	Mmmm.
Lachman:	Okay. Obviously right now you're not under the influence of any sedatives?
Solomon:	Nope.
Lachman:	It's not affecting your judgment or…
Solomon:	Nope. Nope.
Lachman:	Or your thoughts or anything?
Solomon:	Nope.
Lachman:	Okay. And at the time you just told me that you were aware of what was going on when this happened.

Solomon:	Yeah.
Lachman:	That you were perfectly aware of what was going on and…
Solomon:	Yeah.
Lachman:	And you remember what was going on?
Solomon:	Yeah.
Lachman:	And that you weren't zonked out from this medication or anything at this time?
Solomon:	Nope.
Lachman:	Okay. Currently under the care of a psychiatrist or psychologist?
Solomon:	Neither one of 'em (inaudible) me. I'm gonna tell that's the truth. I'm gonna tell you the truth though. I'm not gonna tell you anything false.
Lachman:	You're not currently suffering from any mental illness or diseases?
Solomon:	Nuh uh. (Inaudible) gonna shock you. And that's the truth.
Lachman:	Let me read this to you. As a matter of fact, you're a smart man, why don't you read it yourself? Okay? Read this sentence for me.
Solomon:	Before any questions are asked, I'm advising you of your constitutional rights. You have the right to remain silent. Anything you say may be used against you. You have the right to a lawyer before or during questioning. If you cannot afford a lawyer one will be appointed to you. Uh, I know that. Yeah.
Lachman:	Before any questions are asked I'm advising you of your constitutional rights. You have the right to remain silent. Do you understand that?

Solomon:	Yeah.
Lachman:	Okay, if you understand that I need you to put your initials on the line next to it.
Solomon:	Nah. No.
Lachman:	You don't understand it?
Solomon:	Nah. Before any questions are asked...
Lachman:	Okay. I'm reading this line; you have the right to remain silent. Do you understand that?
Solomon:	What?
Lachman:	Do you understand that?
Solomon:	Yeah.
Lachman:	What does that mean?
Solomon:	Uh, nah. I don't understand. No, I don't.
Lachman:	Okay.
Solomon:	So explain it to me. No, I don't.
Lachman:	You have the right to remain silent. You don't understand that?
Solomon:	Um, um.
Lachman:	Okay. That means that you have the right, right now, not to say anything.
Solomon:	I'm gonna say what's the truth. Yeah.
Lachman:	Okay, what I'm saying is (inaudible) you understand that you have the right not to say anything right now. Do you understand that?
Solomon:	Right. Right, I understand your sense, what. Okay, I understand your sense, what.
Lachman:	Okay.
Solomon:	I'm just gonna tell you the truth about what happened.
Lachman:	Okay. I know, but I've got to make sure you understand your rights.
Solomon:	But I'm not gonna sign anything.

Lachman:	I've got to make sure you understand your rights first.
Solomon:	Okay. Okay.
Lachman:	You can't say anything until—until you understand your rights, okay?
Solomon:	Okay.
Lachman:	You have the right to remain silent, means that at this point in time Rodney Solomon is sitting in this chair right across from me and you have the absolute right, your constitutional right, not to say anything to Detective Martin or me right now and to be quiet. Do you understand that?
Solomon:	Right.
Lachman:	Right, meaning that you understand that?
Solomon:	Right, I understand all right. All right. Cool. I'm gonna tell you everything that happened.
Lachman:	Don't. The only thing I want you to do, if you understand this, I want you to put your initials on the line next to it.
Martin:	It's on time. I mean I'm not trying to trick you or anything.
Lachman:	What's the difference?
Solomon:	All right.
Lachman:	Okay, anything you say may be used against you. What does that mean?
Solomon:	Anything that I say could be used against me. But I'm gonna tell you the truth in court.
Lachman:	Right. Okay, you have the right to have a lawyer before and during questioning. Do you understand that?

Solomon: Why can't I get a lawyer now? Why can't he be here now while I'm tellin' ya'll the truth?

Lachman: Okay.

Martin: Do you want one?

Lachman: If you want one, you can have one here and we end questioning right now and not say another word to you. Do you understand that?

Solomon: Yeah, but see what I'm sayin' is I'm gonna tell you all the exactly the truth of what happened.

Lachman: Okay.

Solomon: It's plain and simple 'cause...

Lachman: Well...

Solomon: His clothes will demonstrate that.

Lachman: Okay.

Solomon: When you all caught him he didn't have 'em on no more. No drawers, no sweatpants.

Lachman: All right.

Solomon: Okay.

Lachman: Right—right now, Rodney, right now you're here without a lawyer. Okay?

Solomon: Uh huh.

Lachman: There's no lawyer here, okay?

Solomon: I'll tell you exactly...

Lachman: Downstairs you told me you wanted to talk to me without a lawyer being present.

Solomon: All right. All right. Okay. Okay. All right.

Lachman: Now it's perfectly up to you. I mean if you tell me, Detective Lachman, I don't want to talk to you until I have a lawyer here...

Solomon: I'll talk to you right now. I'll talk to you right now.

Lachman:	I'll take you back downstairs it doesn't matter to me.
Solomon:	I'll talk to you right now. Come on.
Lachman:	So, you want to talk to me without a lawyer?
Solomon:	Yeah, yeah.
Lachman:	Okay. Will you put your initials next to the line saying you understand it? If you cannot afford a lawyer, one will be appointed for you.
Solomon:	I can't afford one.
Lachman:	Right. Do you understand that?
Solomon:	Yeah.
Lachman:	And if you can't afford one, one will be appointed for you and if you wanted one today, or before you wanted to talk to the police, the court would appoint one for you. Do you understand that?
Solomon:	Yeah. Listen, Detective, all's I'm sayin' is right.
Lachman:	You gotta finish this first.
Solomon:	Okay, come on.
Lachman:	We gotta finish this first.
Martin:	Okay, sign there if you understand that right.
Solomon:	I can't afford no lawyer now.
Lachman:	Right. And you understand that I want you to understand that just because you can't afford a lawyer, just because you can't afford one, doesn't mean that's why you're talkin' to us now. Do you know what I'm sayin'?
Solomon:	I'll talk to ya'll now and when I get a lawyer.
Lachman:	Okay, so I just want you to understand that.
Solomon:	All right.

Lachman:	Okay. Now the next question is, do you understand your rights as explained? Which means, do you understand the information that I just explained to you? If you understand it, I need you to circle yes and put your initials on the line above that. I need you to circle yes if you understand it.
Martin:	Do you understand the rights as were just explained to you?
Lachman:	That's the only thing I'm askin', okay? Having been advised of your rights, having us explain some information, are you willing to answer questions now?
Solomon:	I'm willing to answer questions. I'm willing. Yes. Yeah. Yeah. Whatever.
Lachman:	If you understand that I need you to circle yes and put your initials on the line above that.
Martin:	Sign your name and we're done.
Solomon:	Yeah.
Lachman:	Sign your name down there. Is that your regular signature?
Solomon:	Mmmm.
Lachman:	Do you want to sign that, Detective Martin?
Solomon:	Let's see. Once I tell you exactly what actually happened…
Martin:	Okay. Let's start off—let's start off…
Solomon:	You'll believe me more than you believe him. I'm gonna tell you why.
Lachman:	Let's start off from the beginning.
Solomon:	I'm gonna tell you why.
Lachman:	Okay, when did you all hook up this morning?
Solomon:	Uh, early this morning.

Lachman:	About what time?
Solomon:	Uh, I guess about four.
Lachman:	Four. Where'd you hook up with them?
Solomon:	Uh, on 95. You know, like East Capitol Street.
Lachman:	East Capitol Street?
Solomon:	Yeah.
Lachman:	Who all was in your group?
Solomon:	Me and him and my little buddy. She a good friend of mine. I want to take her back and…
Lachman:	Okay. So, the person that was with you in the car at that time and when the police caught you…
Solomon:	Yeah. Yeah.
Lachman:	Who else?
Solomon:	And little Shawn…
Lachman:	Little Shawn?
Solomon:	She was the one that was out…
Lachman:	Okay. Okay. And whose car were you in?
Solomon:	Uh, his friend's car.
Lachman:	His friend's car?
Solomon:	Mmmm.
Lachman:	And what was his friend's name?
Solomon:	Uh, I think they call him… He got a nickname or somethin' they call him.
Lachman:	Okay.
Solomon:	Anyway…
Lachman:	What kind of car was it?
Solomon:	It was a—a—a…
Lachman:	Cadillac?
Solomon:	Yeah. No.
Lachman:	All right. So, when you all hooked up, what was the purpose of ya'll gettin' together?

Solomon:	Take her back to… We was ridin' together.
Lachman:	Take her? Being?
Solomon:	I was drivin' with him.
Lachman:	Okay, so he's driving.
Solomon:	Yeah.
Lachman:	Okay, and you were ridin' with him. And who else was in the car? You're takin' who to Job Corps?
Solomon:	Her. LaShawn.
Lachman:	LaShawn. Okay, and what happened when you went to take her to Job Corps?
Solomon:	Uh, he got lost. He got lost, right?
Lachman:	Okay.
Solomon:	So, the car we was drivin'—he was drivin', ran out of gas. So he took the key out, right? Out the ignition, right? And gave to me so I was lookin' for a gas can. So, I popped the trunk lid lookin' for a gas can. So I didn't see one. So, I put a key back in my pocket, right back. We drove to the phone. Try to use the phone to see if we can call somebody. So that didn't work, right?
Lachman:	Why didn't that work? Nobody was home?
Solomon:	Yeah, nobody was home.
Lachman:	Okay, but the phone worked?
Solomon:	Yeah, the phone worked.
Lachman:	Okay, so nobody was home.
Solomon:	He started sayin', uh yeah, we gonna get a car. Come on we gonna get a car the best way we can. Come on. Come on with me. So I walked with him. We walked and walked and walked, right? And then we see this lady, right; he pulls up on the lady.
Lachman:	Uh huh.

Solomon: She stops before…
Lachman: Pulls up on her? What do you mean by that?
Solomon: You know he pulled up on her. He asked her, he say…
Lachman: He walked? Did he walk up to her?
Solomon: Yeah, while she was in the car. She was in the car.
Lachman: She was in the car.
Solomon: Yeah. I'm standin' maybe 15 feet away. You know, wait to see people crowdin', movin' in to get the car (inaudible) 'cause he said hold on (inaudible). Listen, listen. He opened up the door. He snatched the lady out, right? Right? The lady was not… The lady was still halfway in it. Still holdin' on to the door.
Lachman: Right.
Solomon: So he jumps in the driver's side. I jumped in the other side. He said to me, come on. Come on, man. Come on.
Lachman: Okay.
Solomon: While the lady is still holdin' the door he drives. He tries to push her out.
Lachman: Okay.
Solomon: She still draggin'. (Inaudible) I was tryin' to get him to stop. He stops. He tried to push her out there.
Lachman: Uh huh.
Solomon: But all (inaudible) sweatpants. See I noticed when you locked him up he didn't have on his sweatpants. He didn't have any pants on. I did.
Lachman: Okay.
Solomon: Then he borrowed my pants.

Lachman: So, tell me what happened.
Solomon: Then he stopped, pushed her off. You know, she got off. He pushed her off, right? Then he took the little baby that was in the back.
Lachman: Okay.
Solomon: He grabbed the baby and put the little baby out and said, come on, man. Come on. Come on. He started drivin'. So, when we got to a gas station he said, man, since you the oldest, you drive. He said man; I ain't got no license. He said well you's older, so you drive.
Lachman: Uh huh.
Solomon: We got to the station I just started drivin'. This (inaudible), okay?
Lachman: Now...
Solomon: If (inaudible) could should you. Take a blood test. There's no blood on my clothes. Nowhere on my clothes. Am I right or wrong, Detective?
Lachman: Well, I don't know, I haven't tested 'em yet.
Solomon: There's no blood on 'em.
Lachman: There's (inaudible) it's hard to tell. You know...
Solomon: It's not on those.
Lachman: You understand...
Solomon: Just hands, my head (inaudible) sweatpants on.
Lachman: Uh huh.
Solomon: Did you ever find 'em?
Lachman: Well, we're still workin' on that.

Solomon:	He threw 'em away because they so much blood on 'em. He threw 'em out the window.
Lachman:	Where?
Solomon:	On the highway somewhere. You know, while he was drivin' he was throwin' off the… They got too much blood on 'em. I'm throwin' these away.
Lachman:	Was that before you went to the car wash and got all the blood washed off?
Solomon:	Yeah.
Lachman:	You were drivin' at the car wash?
Solomon:	That's when we switched.
Lachman:	At the car wash?
Solomon:	Just before we got to the car wash we switched up.
Lachman:	Where'd you pull off the side of the road?
Solomon:	Yeah. He said why don't you drive since you got a license.
Lachman:	Mmmm. And then you were the one drivin'?
Solomon:	He said I'm older.
Lachman:	You were the one drivin' at the car wash?
Solomon:	Yeah.
Lachman:	Okay, you drove up and you were in the passenger—driver's seat?
Solomon:	Yeah.
Lachman:	Okay, and you were wearin' a Redskins shirt?
Solomon:	Yeah.
Lachman:	And you were the one that was trying to buy the guy's watch?
Solomon:	Yeah.
Lachman:	Okay.

Solomon:	Yeah, I had a lot (inaudible).
Lachman:	So, what happened after you left the car wash?
Solomon:	We was drivin'. We was drivin'. We was drivin' and that's when and that's when we found out the police was comin' after us. I said—he said, man the police (inaudible). Then I said, well fuck it. We pulled over. We tried to—I was chasin' (inaudible). When he got away all he had was his drawers on.
Lachman:	So, when you ran in…
Solomon:	I had my clothes on.
Lachman:	The police were chasin' you, right?
Solomon:	Yeah. I fell in the mud. Yeah.
Lachman:	You fell in the mud?
Solomon:	Yeah.
Lachman:	And when you came out of the woods the helicopter was there?
Solomon:	Yeah.
Lachman:	And the guy from the helicopter jumped out and grabbed you?
Solomon:	Yeah. I stopped. I stopped him.
Lachman:	Yeah.
Solomon:	Yeah.
Lachman:	Well, you can't outrun a helicopter now, can you?
Solomon:	Yeah.
Lachman:	Okay. (Inaudible).
Solomon:	Yeah.
Lachman:	All right. So, let's go over this from the time you ran out of gas, okay? So, when you went to walk down into that housing

	community, what was the first thing that you did when you got down there?
Solomon:	He said, he said, he said, come on, man, I'm gonna ask one of these people can we use their phone. Come on. Come on. And then he asked—he asked the lady.
Lachman:	Did he ask somebody…
Solomon:	He asked the lady. He asked the lady. She said no; she wouldn't let him use the phone.
Lachman:	Okay, was this a different lady?
Solomon:	Yeah.
Lachman:	He asked a different lady if he could use the phone?
Solomon:	Yeah.
Lachman:	What did she look like?
Solomon:	I don't remember what she looked like. Stuff happened so fast, right? Man, you know.
Lachman:	Did it?
Solomon:	Yeah.
Lachman:	So, did that lady have a car? The first lady that you asked if you could use the phone?
Solomon:	I think she had a truck or somethin'. Car or van or somethin'. Yeah.
Lachman:	A van?
Solomon:	Yeah.
Lachman:	Do you know what color that was?
Solomon:	Like gray.
Lachman:	Gray.
Solomon:	Yeah.
Lachman:	Who went up and talked to her, him or you?
Solomon:	After, after he asked if he could use the phone, she said the lady down the street might let us use it. Then I asked her… I

	went to her after that, said you think the lady'd let us use it. So she said no. No. No. I said okay.
Lachman:	Okay. So, after that happened, what did you all do?
Solomon:	We walked. We walked. We walked down the—to the next um town complex.
Lachman:	Okay.
Solomon:	And then the BMW. The lady was like she was ready to get into her BMW. Put—laid the child in the top. So I'm standin' back. Come on. Come on.
Lachman:	Did you all walk by her as she was gettin' in the car?
Solomon:	Yeah.
Lachman:	You were walkin' in front of him.
Solomon:	Yeah.
Lachman:	You know why I knew that?
Solomon:	No.
Lachman:	Because we saw it on videotape.
Solomon:	You did?
Lachman:	Yeah. Her husband was standin' inside and videotaped the whole thing.
Solomon:	Yeah?
Lachman:	You were walkin' in front of him and you had a jacket up around your face.
Solomon:	No, it wasn't on my face. It was…
Lachman:	Yeah. I wouldn't have known that if I didn't have a videotape now, would I?
Solomon:	Yeah, I was sweatin'.
Lachman:	And he was walkin' behind you. He was walkin' about…
Solomon:	You didn't videotape him talkin' to her?
Lachman:	The entire thing.

Solomon: Yeah. Did he videotape the entire thing?
Lachman: Why don't we go over what actually happened?
Solomon: That's what I'm tellin' you. Did he videotape the entire thing?
Lachman: Why don't we go over what actually happened?
Solomon: I'm tellin' you what actually happened. He pulled out the car. He did it.
Lachman: You also got into that door.
Solomon: No. Then I went around the other door, 'cause he drove. Then he pulled off first. He pulled—he drove it off.
Lachman: You were there when the whole thing happened. You were right there.
Solomon: Yeah, but he was pullin' her. He was...
Lachman: You were right next to him.
Solomon: Yeah, but he was doin' (inaudible) blood got on him.
Lachman: All of the blood got on him?
Solomon: Yeah.
Lachman: You were right there with him.
Solomon: Yeah, I was there when this happened. Yeah.
Lachman: You guys...
Solomon: I'm just tryin' to let you know who doin' most the work.
Lachman: I know. I know you got in the same door as he did.
Solomon: I had to.
Lachman: You told me you got in the passenger's door.
Solomon: No. I said when we switched. When we switched. When we switched drivin'...

Lachman:	That's when you got in…
Solomon:	Yeah.
Lachman:	When you were standin' there, when the lady was being wrestled with, you all got in the same door.
Solomon:	Yeah.
Lachman:	You both got in the driver's door with her hangin' there…
Solomon:	Yeah, 'cause he was up.
Lachman:	With her hangin' there, right?
Solomon:	Yeah.
Lachman:	You both got in the car and you were like sittin' on top of him when you drove off.
Solomon:	No, he took off.
Lachman:	You were with him though.
Solomon:	Yeah, I was right with 'em.
Lachman:	In the same seat almost?
Solomon:	Almost. Almost, yeah. He was still tryin' to push her out.
Lachman:	Right.
Solomon:	And the door was hittin' her. The door—she was draggin on the—he said you got that (inaudible).
Lachman:	And where were you?
Solomon:	Uh, I was in the other seat then.
Lachman:	You were over on the other seat by then?
Solomon:	Yeah.
Lachman:	Okay. And then when you all hit the fence…
Solomon:	Uh, he—he almost hit the fence. Yeah.
Lachman:	Almost?
Solomon:	He did, didn't he?
Lachman:	You were there, you tell me.
Solomon:	He did. He was drivin'.

Lachman:	Was that an accident that you hit the fence?
Solomon:	He did it…
Lachman:	Okay.
Solomon:	Got all that on videocassette, huh? Yeah.
Lachman:	So basically—basically, although you knew he was gonna take the car, you got in…
Solomon:	Yeah, I got in.
Lachman:	Gettin' in the car (inaudible).
Solomon:	So I could get a ride home. Yeah.
Lachman:	You got in the car, right?
Solomon:	Yeah.
Lachman:	Right. So, you'd get the car, right?
Solomon:	No, I wasn't… My, my, my, my, my, logic to the whole—the whole…
Lachman:	You all wanted the lady's car to go back to D.C.
Solomon:	Yeah.
Lachman:	Right.
Solomon:	He said come on get in the car. Then he said he wanted…
Lachman:	Right. And you went with him?
Solomon:	Yeah, I went with 'em. Yeah.
Lachman:	Okay.
Solomon:	Tell you what happened. I'm just lettin' you know who did most of the work.
Lachman:	Most of the work?
Solomon:	Yeah.
Lachman:	You were there though.
Solomon:	Yeah.
Lachman:	You were helpin' him.
Solomon:	No, but if he (inaudible) killin' that woman. Who killed that woman?
Lachman:	Well that's like I said, I want you to tell me from your perspective…

Solomon:	Who killed that woman?
Lachman:	I want you to tell me from your perspective.
Solomon:	Ya'll not stupid. I'm not stupid.
Lachman:	Right.
Solomon:	If she dragged in the street, he pushin' and still pushin' while he was drivin'.
Lachman:	Okay, then what happened when you were going down the road? How did she finally get off the car?
Solomon:	He took her, um, seatbelt off her arm. It was like connect to her, um, wrist.
Lachman:	In other words, just explain to me what happened when you all pulled out of that road. What happened? Step by step.
Solomon:	What you mean?
Lachman:	When you pulled out of the road with her draggin', what happened?
Solomon:	Yeah.
Lachman:	Was the baby crying?
Solomon:	Yeah.
Lachman:	Was the baby screaming?
Solomon:	He said come on, baby, I'm gonna stop. I'm gonna get this baby outta here. He was tellin' me he was gonna get this baby outta here. He was tellin' me get the baby outta here.
Lachman:	Okay. Now, when she was being wrestled with, when the car was being taken, was she saying anything?
Solomon:	She was hollerin' and screamin', yeah.
Lachman:	What was she screamin'?
Solomon:	Somethin' about the baby.
Lachman:	Like what? Tell me for example.
Solomon:	Don't hurt her baby or somethin'

Lachman:	Don't hurt the baby?
Solomon:	Yeah.
Lachman:	So, she was wrestling with you 'cause she didn't want you to take off with her baby.
Solomon:	Yeah.
Lachman:	Is that right?
Solomon:	Yeah, you right.
Lachman:	Okay. And when you all were pullin' off, I mean she was being dragged, was she screamin'?
Solomon:	Yeah, she was.
Lachman:	Was she? How was she screamin'?
Solomon:	Callin', makin' noise. He was still tryin' to push her out the door while he was drivin'. He was drivin'.
Lachman:	What part of her was inside the door?
Solomon:	Like her hand was still closed in the door.
Lachman:	Was it her arm or her hand?
Solomon:	This part.
Lachman:	That part of her hand, like from the wrist down.
Solomon:	Yeah, yeah. I was sittin' on the other seat while he was drivin'.
Lachman:	You pointed to her right hand.
Solomon:	Yeah, it was her right hand.
Lachman:	It was her right hand?
Solomon:	Yeah.
Lachman:	Okay, and what were you doing?
Solomon:	I was tellin' him man you shouldn't do that. Man, come on, man. You fucked up, man. We didn't had to go get it like this. We should just make a phone call. We didn't had to go try to go home like this.

Lachman:	Now, when you pulled out of the street, how long was it before you hit the fence?
Solomon:	Uh, say it again. Run that back to me. I…
Lachman:	When you pulled out of the street, draggin' the lady, at what point did you hit the fence?
Solomon:	A few minutes later. A few minutes later.
Lachman:	A few minutes later?
Solomon:	He was drivin'. Yeah.
Lachman:	He was drivin' when you hit the fence?
Solomon:	Yeah.
Lachman:	Okay, and what happened after you hit the fence?
Solomon:	He put it in reverse. You know, pulled back.
Lachman:	Then what happened after that? What did you do after that?
Solomon:	We pulled over. He said you—he said you the oldest, you drive.
Lachman:	How long was it before you pulled over? That's what I'm saying.
Solomon:	Not that long.
Lachman:	Was she still dragging when you pulled over?
Solomon:	Yeah. Yeah.
Lachman:	What happened then?
Solomon:	He took the seatbelt thing off her arm and then that's it. And unhooked it—let her in the street. He did.
Lachman:	When did you all take the baby out of the car?
Solomon:	Uh, right after.
Lachman:	Right after you did what?
Solomon:	Got rid of her.
Lachman:	After you got rid of her?

Solomon:	Yeah, after he got rid of her off the thing. Yeah.
Lachman:	You were right at the same place, or after you pulled off.
Solomon:	After we pulled off.
Lachman:	What happened after you pulled off?
Solomon:	Nothin'. We was goin' too fast now.
Lachman:	After you pulled off from the lady, the baby's in the car, right? Where was the baby in the car?
Solomon:	In the backseat.
Lachman:	Behind the driver or the passenger?
Solomon:	In the backseat of the car. But I'm tellin' ya she was in the car seat.
Lachman:	Right. In other words, was the baby behind the driver or the passenger?
Solomon:	Behind my side.
Lachman:	Your side?
Solomon:	Behind me. Yeah.
Lachman:	And when you pulled off, how long was it before you stopped and the baby was taken out of the car?
Solomon:	A couple of minutes.
Lachman:	And who took the baby out of the car?
Solomon:	He did.
Lachman:	And how did he take the baby out of the car?
Solomon:	He stopped and he took the, you know, the car seat loop.
Lachman:	And how did he take the baby out and set it down? Did he take the baby seat and throw it or what?
Solomon:	He like dropped it down.
Lachman:	Just dropped it?
Solomon:	Yeah. Then he said you drive. You know.

Lachman:	He asked you to drive?
Solomon:	Yeah.
Lachman:	Then what happened?
Solomon:	Then I drove. Started drivin', right? And I said he said man why don't you go to the car wash man. So we stopped throwin'—start throwin' all the stuff away that had blood on it. He started—had blood on it and nothin' I had had blood on it.
Lachman:	Did you all go through her purse?
Solomon:	He did.
Lachman:	He did?
Solomon:	Mmmm.
Lachman:	What did the purse look like?
Solomon:	I don't know he threw it away. I asked him. He threw it away.
Lachman:	Did you take anything out of it?
Solomon:	I think he took some credit cards out of it.
Lachman:	Credit cards?
Solomon:	Mmmm.
Lachman:	Did he take anything else?
Solomon:	No.
Lachman:	Did he look through anything else?
Solomon:	I don't know I wasn't payin' attention. I was drivin' then.
Lachman:	You were drivin'.
Solomon:	Yeah.
Lachman:	Did you throw anything out the window?
Solomon:	Nope.
Lachman:	Ever? You never threw anything out the window?
Solomon:	I might throw a piece of napkin that was on the side right there.

Lachman:	What about her shoe? Got a lady that was sitting at a stop light right down the…
Solomon:	I put one shoe…
Lachman:	She was driving. You put the shoe out the window and the woman told you, you threw the shoes out the window.
Solomon:	It was one shoe.
Lachman:	Yeah, remember that?
Solomon:	I did. I was drivin' then.
Lachman:	You were drivin' then, right?
Solomon:	Yeah. When that lady talked to you and told you (inaudible).
Lachman:	Right.
Solomon:	Yeah, you know. Yeah.
Lachman:	Then what happened? After you pulled through the light?
Solomon:	(Inaudible) we gotta go get the car washed. You know, make sure the car, you know isn't dirty. It's all cleaned, you know.
Lachman:	Get all the blood and all that off…
Solomon:	Yeah. He had all this blood on his hand.
Lachman:	Was there a lot of… Was there a lot of flesh and stuff on the car too?
Solomon:	A little bit.
Lachman:	Blood?
Solomon:	A little bit.
Lachman:	Okay. And you said you drove to the car wash?
Solomon:	Yeah, I did. We switched there.
Lachman:	So, you didn't just switch right before you got to the car wash? You switched a long time before that?

Solomon:	No. Wasn't much longer before… He was the one wrecked it, remember? He ran by the fence.
Lachman:	Let's put it this way, you had switched before you got to the stoplight where you threw the shoe out the window, right?
Solomon:	Yeah.
Lachman:	Right. Then after that you all drove to the car wash.
Solomon:	No, I was drivin' then.
Lachman:	That's a pretty long way to the car wash.
Solomon:	Yeah.
Lachman:	I mean we're talkin' a good half-hour drive there. It depends on how fast you're goin'. How fast were you goin'?
Solomon:	About 60 miles an hour.
Lachman:	Sixty? Okay, so you drove to the car wash. Did you just stumble across it? Were you lost?
Solomon:	No, I wasn't lost.
Lachman:	You knew where you were going? Where were you when you had the car washed?
Solomon:	No, I didn't know where I was goin' until…
Lachman:	So, if you don't know where you're goin', you're lost.
Solomon:	Yeah.
Lachman:	Were you lost?
Solomon:	Yeah, 'cause I think if I had got on the beltway we probably would have been all right.
Lachman:	Okay.
Solomon:	Wouldn't we?
Lachman:	Yeah, you were all right. You were a long way from the beltway.

Solomon:	I know.
Lachman:	So you went to the car wash?
Solomon:	Yeah.
Lachman:	You pulled up to the car wash and the guy is standing there?
Solomon:	Yeah, and that's when…
Lachman:	And you told him it was an accident or something?
Solomon:	Yeah. That's when I asked about a wash.
Lachman:	Okay.
Solomon:	I (inaudible).
Lachman:	What did you tell him about the stuff on the car?
Solomon:	I said somethin' I don't remember. I got… That's what happened so fast. I not gonna lie.
Lachman:	Didn't you ask him to clean the rear wheel too?
Solomon:	Yeah.
Lachman:	Because there was stuff on the wheel too?
Solomon:	Yeah.
Lachman:	And then you went through the car wash?
Solomon:	Right.
Lachman:	What happened after you left the car wash?
Solomon:	Then we pulled off. I was drivin' then.
Lachman:	You were drivin'. Okay.
Solomon:	That's what I say. After that I noticed… I thought it was from D. C.
Lachman:	Uh huh.
Solomon:	And they was lookin' for… The dude at the gas station told us they lookin' for a stolen BMW Grandville. And then I saw the cop behind me.
Lachman:	You saw the cop behind you?

Solomon:	Yeah, I seen him.
Lachman:	What did you do when you saw him behind you?
Solomon:	Sped up a little bit, that's what.
Lachman:	What happened next?
Solomon:	Then I was by somebody at the light. They had a like a block tryin' to block me off, huh.
Lachman:	Right. Then what did you do?
Solomon:	Back up.
Lachman:	Speeding?
Solomon:	Yeah, speedin' up. Yeah. That's when I got all the mud. That's when I got all the mud.
Lachman:	Okay, that's when you…
Solomon:	He—he didn't run. He didn't have anything to run in. He didn't have no pants or nothin' there.
Lachman:	It's kinda hard runnin' in shorts ain't it?
Solomon:	Yeah. He had—he had on drawers.
Lachman:	Now, when you were backin' up, what made you lose control of the car?
Solomon:	Speed. Speedin'.
Lachman:	And that's when you hit that embankment and went out in the cow field?
Solomon:	Yeah.
Lachman:	All right. Then you jumped out of the car and you were in the driver's seat?
Solomon:	Yeah.
Lachman:	You jumped out of the car and you ran?
Solomon:	Yeah.
Lachman:	Then he got caught right there at the car. You were tellin' him to run though, weren't you?
Solomon:	Yeah.

Lachman:	And then the officers were chasin' you and that's when you ran into that big mud thing, right?
Solomon:	Mmmm.
Lachman:	And the officer was right behind you in the mud and when you got out of the mud, that's when the helicopter got you, right?
Solomon:	Right.
Lachman:	Okay and the helicopter guy got out of the helicopter?
Solomon:	Can you answer this though?
Lachman:	Rodney, right?
Solomon:	Okay, let me ask you this. Okay, no matter what statement he made and no matter what statement I made, right? Listen; was I the whole scene on the videotape? What happened?
Lachman:	There.
Solomon:	Okay, I'm cool with that. That's all I wanted to know.
Lachman:	All right. How about the…
Solomon:	I ain't in bad shape, you know. Now.
Lachman:	You hit the rest area. Do you remember going to the rest area?
Solomon:	Yeah, I ain't in bad shape, am I? I ain't in that much bad of a shape. Tell the truth on the videotape.
Lachman:	Well, like I said, you know a lot about the law.
Solomon:	Yeah.
Lachman:	What's the law when something like that happens?
Solomon:	I don't follow what you're sayin'.

Lachman:	Obviously. What do you know about the law? What do you know about the law when two people do something together—at the same time, knowing that something like that is going to go on?
Solomon:	Oh, I got aiding and abetting. But he was the cause of it. I know he was. He was the main…
Lachman:	So, in other words, what I'm sayin' is…
Solomon:	I was with him.
Lachman:	You were with him.
Solomon:	Right.
Lachman:	He knew he was gonna steal the car from the woman.
Solomon:	Right. Right. Right.
Lachman:	You went out there with him.
Solomon:	Right.
Lachman:	You got in the car with him after you saw all of that go on and you all drove away.
Solomon:	I started though… You know what though, I started gettin' out of the car and hitchhike. I did.
Lachman:	You started to. That's not… I wouldn't say anything about that.
Solomon:	No, I was thinkin' about it in my mind. You know. You know.
Lachman:	Thought about it in your mind.
Solomon:	Yep. Yep.
Lachman:	It didn't show in your actions.

The interview with Rodney Solomon concluded at about 5:25 PM and the tape recorder was turned off. At that time Solomon made the comment, "I probably won't be around." Believing that he was saying he would attempt to take his life, the recorder was again turned on. Solomon then said, "I was just playin'."

Rodney Solomon was returned to his cell to await transport to the District Court Commissioner for a bond review hearing.

Ten

Bernard Eric Miller was taken from his cell to be fingerprinted and photographed prior to his scheduled bond hearing. While being processed, the young man who only hours earlier had been arrested for his part in the murder of Pam Basu, brazenly said, "When are you gonna hurry and get this over with so I can call my mother and go home."

While detectives made preparations to take Miller and Solomon to the District Court Commissioner other problems began to arise. By now the carjacking death of Doctor Pam Basu was not only making headlines locally, but also nationwide. The broadcasts gave detailed accounts of the incident, including the throwing of 22-month-old Sarina from the car.

Inmates at the Howard County Detention Center watched the news coverage with special interest. Even among the most hardened criminals there exists an unwritten code of ethics. The vast majority of prison inmates take a dim view of those who mistreat, molest or abuse children and, in the eyes of many; this act of barbarity crossed the line.

Shortly after the news broadcasts began, talk circulated within the Howard County Police Department about anonymous telephone calls being received there and at the court commissioner's office threatening the lives of Solomon and Miller. An informed source from the detention center reported that rumors circled quickly that harm would come to them when they were turned out into the general population at the jail. And, due to the nature of the crime with which they were charged, it was a certainty they would be sent to the detention center.

Detectives John Hall and Joseph Geibler were assigned to take Rodney Solomon to the Howard County District Court Commissioner for his initial appearance. During the hearing before District Court Commissioner Lewis, Solomon fell asleep several times and had to be awakened by either Commissioner Lewis raising his voice, or by Detective Geibler shaking his shoulder. Commissioner Lewis' questions of Solomon were met with a belligerent response. At one point when asked a question, Solomon snapped, "You've got it all right in front of you." At the conclusion of the hearing he stood up and said, "That's all right, this is all because of this racist county."

Detectives Hall and Geibler transported Rodney Solomon to the Howard County Detention Center and turned him over to Corrections Department Personnel. As Hall and Geibler were preparing to leave the jail, Hall turned to answer a question asked by one of the guards. While talking with the guard, Hall was able to observe Solomon through the observation window of the holding cell. At that time Solomon pulled his penis from his pants and began shaking it with his right hand while looking at Hall. He looked from Hall to his penis and back several times to be sure that Hall was watching what he was doing.

The shaking of his penis at Detective John Hall was only the beginning of acts of defiance by Rodney Solomon. He would employ many tactics in an attempt to defile and intimidate those around him. He began by informing guards, "I'm gonna fuck everybody up." His continued behavior would later cause one Corrections Officer to say, "Even an animal wouldn't lower itself to Rodney Solomon's level."

A source within the Department of Corrections said it was only an act on his part to keep from being placed within the general population where other inmates could get at him. He put up a front because he feared for his life and the louder and more boisterous his act; the less likely it was for him to be sent among the general populace.

In the end, Solomon's act would ensure his wish. He and Bernard Miller would be placed in special isolation cells; safe from the rumored retribution by convicted criminals who viewed their moral standards to be higher than those of the accused killers.

***

In a house not so many miles from the detention center, Steve Basu struggled to find some logic in the maze of insanity that swirled around him. A day full of bright sunshine and an almost dizzying happiness over Sarina's first day of pre-school ended with clouds of despair. In a senseless moment of greed, a brutal act would leave him a widower and a father asking himself how he could possibly summon the strength to go on, and alone raise a child he and Pam had adopted. He would suffer through many long, sleepless nights asking over and over "Why?" but never finding the answer.

Police Officers, Troopers and Detectives involved with the case stopped to question the sheer savagery of this crime. Men and women of law enforcement grow accustomed to dealing with violence and gradually accept it as part of their daily lives. However, this particular act was committed with such barbaric cruelty that even the toughest cops would shake their heads in disbelief and ask "Why?"

Officer Jody Tookey slept very little that night. Visions of the day's events would invade her sleep and haunt her throughout the night. It would be several days before she would again sleep soundly, but then only from exhaustion. Sometime later, during an interview with Fox 5 Television's Hillary Howard, she said, "Nobody deserves to die like that."

For investigators there would be only a few hours of rest before they again set out in search of additional evidence. It would be a painstaking hunt for clues to help piece together the chain of events that led to the tragic death of Pam Basu.

Detective First Class Frank Dayhoff, along with Cadets Robert Cassell and Steve Willingham conducted a search along the shoulders of the roadway at the point where the body was removed from the car. They began their search at that location on Gorman Road and walked to U. S. Route 29, a distance of several miles.

Dayhoff's report stated, "On 09-09-92 at 11:55 AM, DFC Dayhoff discovered a white tee shirt on the shoulder of Gorman Road, 47 paces west of Martown Road." The shirt is described as follows:

Size:	Large
Brand Name:	Screen Stars Best Shirt
Condition:	Wet, turned inside out
Style:	Short Sleeve T-shirt with design on front and the initials "TJ" in center of the design.

Dayhoff also retrieved Sarina Basu's car seat from Catherine Nehring and turned it over to Crime Scene Technician Doug Read for processing.

At Police Headquarters, Forensic Services Supervisor R. C. Bartley, and CST Doug Read, scoured Pam Basu's BMW for evidence linking Rodney Eugene Solomon and Bernard Eric Miller to the car. Their efforts would produce 24 latent fingerprint lifts from the 1990 BMW, which would be compared to the inked fingerprint impressions of the suspects.

They continued to look over the car with R. C. Bartley finally lying down and sliding under the vehicle near the driver's side rear wheel well. Within the wheel well itself Mr. Bartley made a gruesome discovery. Around the well he saw what he knew to be blood, and within the blood he noticed obvious bone fragments. The rear driver's wheel was then removed from the car and Mr. Bartley and CST Read discovered human hair, which had been pulled through the wheel and was now entwined around the axle of the car.

Mr. Bartley's report provided the following information regarding fingerprint evidence in the case:

> One latent fingerprint present on lift Number One take by CST Read from the driver's side rear door below the window has been identified as a fingerprint of Rodney Eugene Solomon, born December 22, 1965, HCID #129922.
>
> Twenty-two latent fingerprints, one of which is the lower joint area of a finger, and two latent palm prints present on eleven (11) lifts, number two (2) through twelve (12), taken by CST Read from two credit cards located inside the BMW over the driver's sun visor, and from the outside hood and windshield areas of this car, and the inside window of the right front door (passenger's side) have been identified as finger and palm impressions of Bernard Eric Miller, born November 7, 1975, HCID #129923.
>
> Seven latent lifts numbered forty (40) through (48) were lifted by CST Smith from a Cadillac, Tag Number ZLF 024. Two of these latent fingerprints from the rear view mirror, both present on lift forty-six (46), have been identified as the fingerprints of Miller.
>
> Nine latent lifts numbered forty-nine (49) through fifty-seven (57) were lifted by CST Smith from a Chrysler Lebaron, Tag Number WTH 479. One of these latent fingerprints present on lift number forty-nine (49) has been identified as the fingerprint of Solomon.

While investigators were pursuing every aspect of the case, it was discovered that the Maryland Registration Number ZLF 024 displayed on the Cadillac was listed by the Maryland Motor Vehicle Administration as belonging to Robert Wayne Thompson on a 1985 Chevrolet.

Sergeant Carl Layman traced Thompson to the United States Armed Forces, temporarily on duty in Biloxi, Mississippi. Layman contacted Thompson who told him the tags were apparently stolen from his car after it had broken down on the Baltimore-Washington Parkway in May 1992. Thompson had left his car and reported to his duty station, and was unaware of the theft until he was contacted by Sergeant Layman.

At this time the Howard County Police enlisted the aid of the Federal Bureau of Investigation in tracing rightful ownership of the Cadillac. Special Agent Scott Pulver was assigned the task of locating the owner of the car. Pulver located Timothy Levette Robinson in the District of Columbia Jail and interviewed him regarding ownership of the Cadillac.

Robinson told Pulver that he'd purchased a Cadillac approximately two to three weeks prior to the carjacking incident in Howard County. He'd paid $500.00 cash for the vehicle, and an individual he knew as "TJ" provided half of the money. He said "TJ" was a neighbor and they were going to share the car. He also told Special Agent Pulver that "TJ" was currently incarcerated in Howard County for a carjacking incident.

Pulver's investigation concluded that Timothy Levette Robinson and Bernard Eric Miller were co-owners of the 1975 Cadillac.

Eleven

On September 9, 1992 Detective Lee Lachman received a telephone call from McLindzey Hawkins, the Security Supervisor at the Howard County Detention Center. Hawkins told Detective Lachman that he was present while Ms Barbara Brooks from the Classification Division was processing Miller.

During classification inmates are advised of their charges and provided information about the Howard County Detention Center. While they attempted to complete the processing procedures Miller continually changed the topic to the previous day's events. He repeatedly said he wanted to "confess and tell the truth about the incident."

At that time Mr. Hawkins telephoned Detective Lachman and permitted Miller to speak with him. During their conversation Miller told Lachman he wanted to "tell the whole truth and confess."

The following are excerpts taken directly from the taped interview with Bernard Eric Miller.

    Lachman: Okay, what did Rodney tell you on the way to the rest area?

    Miller: He was gonna get another car.

Lachman:	And how did he say he was going to get the car?
Miller:	He was gonna rough it off.
Lachman:	And what does that mean?
Miller:	He was gonna forcibly take it from somebody.
Lachman:	What happened when you got to the rest area?
Miller:	He saw a white man standing drinking in his car.
Lachman:	Okay, he was sitting in his car?
Miller:	Sitting in his car drinking coffee.
Lachman:	Was the car door open?
Miller:	Yes.
Lachman:	And what happened next?
Miller:	Rodney tried to take the man out the car.
Lachman:	And what did Rodney do when he went up to the car?
Miller:	Told the man he was gonna take his car.
Lachman:	Okay, and did Rodney grab the man?
Miller:	Yes.
Lachman:	And did he wrestle with him?
Miller:	No he just… The man started hollerin' for help and Rodney ran off.
Lachman:	Okay, and what happened when Rodney ran off?
Miller:	Both of us ran off. He said he was gonna get another car.

This portion of the interview centers their encounter with encounter Laura Becraft on Jaclyn Court.

Lachman:	What happened next?
Miller:	He walked around the house and waited for the lady to come back out.
Lachman:	Uh huh.

Miller:	He tried to go to the lady to take her keys and the lady said... Started hollerin' for help. Then she said I can identify you.
Lachman:	Okay.
Miller:	Then me and Rodney took off runnin'.
Lachman:	Now, when Rodney went and tried to take her keys, how did he try taking the keys? Did he grab them from her?
Miller:	Yeah, he grabbed the lady's keys.
Lachman:	Did he wrestle back and forth with them?
Miller:	Yeah. She struggled with the keys. He dropped the keys.
Lachman:	Uh huh.
Miller:	Took off runnin'. Ran through some more townhouses.
Lachman:	And then what happened?
Miller:	Me and Rodney took off joggin' through some more townhouses and some woods. Then he said he was gonna rough off another car. Then that's when we saw a brown BMW.
Lachman:	Okay, and rough another car off means what?
Miller:	He was gonna tussle her for her car.
Lachman:	Okay.
Miller:	Forcibly.
Lachman:	And then what happened?
Miller:	Rodney—Rodney forced... Tried to take the lady out her car.
Lachman:	And now when you—you and Rodney went up to the car together, is that right?
Miller:	Yes.

Here Miller again describes the forceful removal of Pam Basu from the car and of her becoming entangled in the seatbelt.

The interview continues at the point where he says they dragged her along Gorman Road, lost control of the car, struck the barbed wire fence and Solomon opened the door.

Lachman:	Okay, and what did you see?
Miller:	I saw the lady hooked to the seatbelt.
Lachman:	And what did she look like?
Miller:	She was red and she—her butt was ripped up and I saw her head.
Lachman:	Which part of her head?
Miller:	The back of her head—messed up.
Lachman:	Was her face facing the ground?
Miller:	Yes.
Lachman:	Okay, and what did—what did her head look like?
Miller:	I saw blood.

At this time Solomon and Miller drove to the point on Gorman Road where Pam Basu was removed from the car and their flight continued.

Lachman:	Okay, and what did you all start doing as soon as you drove off?
Miller:	We just drove farther down the road trying to find the beltway back to Route 70 to get back to D. C.
Lachman:	What did you do with your clothes when you drove off?
Miller:	I—I—I took my shirt off.
Lachman:	Why?
Miller:	'Cause Rodney told me to take my shirt off and get rid of all the evidence.
Lachman:	Okay.
Miller:	He threw my shirt out the driver's side.
Lachman:	Uh huh.
Miller:	I took my pants off. Threw my pants out the passenger's side.

Lachman:	What color were your pants?
Miller:	Red, white and blue.
Lachman:	Your pants were?
Miller:	Yes.
Lachman:	Okay, and did your pants have blood on them?
Miller:	Yes.
Lachman:	Your pants did?
Miller:	At the bottom they was wet. They was wet.
Lachman:	Wet?
Miller:	But you couldn't see no blood or anything 'cause my pants was dark blue.
Lachman:	Uh huh.
Miller:	And they was up here. They was just wet.
Lachman:	All right. Now, your shirt you had on, you got blood on that?
Miller:	Yes, from the back of his hand.
Lachman:	Now, you also got some blood on your shirt when you hit the fence, is that right?
Miller:	Yes.
Lachman:	How did that happen?
Miller:	The window was down and the air was blowin' and it was blowin' inside the car.
Lachman:	There was blood blowing inside?
Miller:	Yes.
Lachman:	You got that on you?
Miller:	Yes.
Lachman:	Okay, what does your shirt look like?
Miller:	It was a white tee shirt.
Lachman:	Did it have anything on it?
Miller:	My name on it. I had TJ on it.
Lachman:	Is that your nickname?
Miller:	Yes.
Lachman:	Why did you take your clothes off?

Miller:	Rodney told me to take my clothes off and get rid of the evidence.
Lachman:	Okay.
Miller:	He threw my shirt out the window.
Lachman:	Uh huh.
Miller:	And I threw my pants out the window.
Lachman:	Did he put anything… Do anything to your shirt before he threw it out the window?
Miller:	He balled it up and threw it out the window.
Lachman:	Did Rodney get anything on him when he snatched the seatbelt off the woman?
Miller:	On his pants was dark black. You couldn't hardly see nothin' on his pants. He kept his clothes on.
Lachman:	Did he get any blood on his hands when he did that?
Miller:	He had blood on my shirt. He had my shirt on his hands.
Lachman:	Mmmm. Did he wipe anything off of his hands on your shirt?
Miller:	No.
Lachman:	So, he threw your shirt out the window?
Miller:	Yes.
Lachman:	What was Rodney telling you after all this happened?
Miller:	He said he was… He said we gonna at least have the car for three days. He was gonna give the… He say know somebody that can change the title and everything over.
Lachman:	Uh huh.
Miller:	He said he was gonna keep the BMW and go to the car wash and get the car washed.
Lachman:	Uh huh.

Miller:	We went to the car wash, got the car washed. It was a tall, light skinned man. Stand—owned—owned... By the 24 hour car wash.
Lachman:	Okay.
Miller:	He washed the car.
Lachman:	Now, he like squirted it off with a hose and then scrubbed it first, didn't he?
Miller:	Yes.
Lachman:	What was he scrubbing?
Miller:	He was scrubbing the side. The side of the car and the tires and the window.
Lachman:	What was he scrubbing off the side of the car?
Miller:	I mean it was stuff. Red stuff on it. Blood.
Lachman:	Okay.
Miller:	He was scrubbin' the car. The man...
Lachman:	Now, when you pulled up to the car wash, who was driving?
Miller:	Rodney.
Lachman:	And what did the man say to you when he saw the stuff on the car?
Miller:	He said, um, what did you all go through. Rodney say we just now come from Atlantic City. He said—he said how'd ya'll crash the car? Rodney say I was drivin' too fast. He say, you know, I was high and everything.
Lachman:	Did Rodney tell him to scrub the tire too?
Miller:	Yes.
Lachman:	Why did he tell him that?
Miller:	The man was just scrubbin' everything and he washed the whole car.
Lachman:	And then you went through the car wash?

Miller: Yes.

Miller tells Lachman of leaving the car wash and going to a gas station where a man tells them the police are looking for a Brown BMW. As they exited the gas station a police car began to pursue them and eventually Rodney Solomon lost control of the car and crashed through a fence.

Lachman: And then what happened?
Miller: And the police… Rodney got out and ran and I stood still. The police locked me up.
Lachman: What did Rodney tell you when you all got out of the car?
Miller: He said—he said he wasn't gonna get locked back up. He said run.
Lachman: Okay, do you think everything was covered pretty thoroughly?
Miller: Yes.
Lachman: Is this the truth about what happened?
Miller: Yes.
Lachman: Okay, are you just telling me this because you think the truth should be known and you want me to know everything about what happened yesterday?
Miller: Yes.
Lachman: Basically you're satisfied with everything we've gone over?
Miller: Yes.
Lachman: You feel comfortable with everything?
Miller: Yes.

The interview concluded at about 12:27 PM on September 9th and Bernard Eric Miller was returned to the custody of detention center personnel.

Twelve

Detective First Class Thomas Martin went to the Office of the Chief Medical Examiner, 111 Penn Street, Baltimore, Maryland and met with Doctor Junaid Shaikh, M.D., and Associate Pathologist. DFC Martin would be present during the autopsy of Doctor Pam Basu, which would be performed by Doctor Shaikh.

The autopsy was completed on September 9, 1992 and the following information was provided to DFC Martin.

Pathologic Diagnoses

I. Multiple Injuries
   A. Head injuries
     1. Partial decapitation of the head involving the fronto-parietal bones and avulsion of the hemispheres of the brain.
     2. Multiple skull fractures, including frontal and left maxillary and nasal bones.
     3. Multiple contusions, abrasions and lacerations of the face and avulsion to the left eye.
   B. Injuries to the torso

1. Multiple abrasions and contusions involving soft tissues.
C. Extremity injuries
1. Fracture distal right humerus; stable dislocation of left elbow joint.
2. Multiple abrasions, contusions and laceration of extremities.
3. Fracture, compound, right distal femur.
4. Bone erosion of right patella, femoral and tibial condyles bilaterally.
5. Dislocation of left ankle joint.
6. Patterned linear abrasions circling proximal part of left arm.
7. Partial dislocation of left shoulder joint.

Opinion:

This 34-year-old Asian Female, Pam Basu, died of severe head injuries sustained while being dragged by her automobile that had been allegedly stolen. The manner of death is **HOMICIDE.** The pattern of injuries indicates that her left arm was trapped by the driver's seatbelt as she was dragged along by the vehicle. She received severe dragging injuries predominantly to the left side of the face, right upper extremity and lower extremities. The abdomen and chest were also injured. The head showed partial decapitation. The deceased had not been consuming alcoholic beverages prior to death.

DFC Martin asked that blood samples be taken and turned over to him in order for comparison tests to be conducted later with bloodstain evidence on the clothing of the suspects. Detective First Class Martin prepared an application for a Search and Seizure Warrant requesting blood, hair and urine samples be taken from Rodney Eugene Solomon and Bernard Eric Miller. Martin's application for the warrant read in part as follows:

"On Tuesday, September 8, 1992 at approximately 8:30 AM an officer from the Howard County Police was alerted by a citizen of a vehicle being driven west on Gorman Road near Forest Ridge Elementary School. According to the citizen it appeared there was a body hanging from the door of the vehicle. The officer proceeded westbound on Gorman Road for approximately one mile. The officer located the body of the victim, Pam Basu, in the 9900 block of Gorman Road. Basu had died of massive head and bodily injuries. The injuries were caused by being dragged along the pavement and the manner of death was ruled a HOMICIDE.

Crime scene analysis revealed blood, bone fragments, hair and brain matter along the road pavement on Gorman Road. Investigation of the crime scene also revealed damage to a wooden post of a barbed wire fence. The fence was located on the left (south) side of Gorman Road a short distance east of where Basu's body was found. There was blood and/or tissue on portions of the fence and barbed wire. Later examination of Basu revealed a portion of the barbed wire wrapped around her body.

A description of the stolen BMW was broadcast via the police radio and a lookout given to the Maryland State Police. At approximately 9:55 AM officers from the State Police and the Howard County Police spotted the stolen BMW on Route 108 and Route 216, Clarksville, Howard County, Maryland. The vehicle was occupied by two suspects. The suspects attempted to elude police and crashed the BMW. The suspects fled the area on foot and were arrested after a short foot chase.

The suspects/defendants were identified as:
1) driver, SOLOMON, RODNEY EUGENE, black male, date of birth 12-22-65
2) passenger, MILLER, BERNARD ERIC, black male, date of birth 11-07-75

Examination of Miller's and Solomon's clothing revealed what appears to be blood and hair on their clothing.

Basu's 1990 BMW, bearing Maryland Registration WMN 492 was taken into police custody and secured. Crime Laboratory Technicians examined the BMW and blood and hair were collected from the BMW.

Your affiant knows from experience that when a body is dragged or thrown from a moving vehicle there is a transfer of blood, tissue and hair. The aforementioned items would splatter and become attached to clothing and to the vehicle. In this type of crime, robbery and assault, where it is known there was contact between the victim, Basu, and the suspects, Miller and Solomon, there is a high probability there was a transfer of blood and hair from Basu to the suspects. Your affiant would therefore like to seize known blood and hair samples from Miller and Solomon for later serology and microscopic analysis.

It is known that both Miller and Solomon have been arrested for drug related offenses in the past. Your affiant knows from experience that criminals who commit crimes of violence to wit: robbery and assault, the act is sometimes drug related. Either the suspect is on drugs or committing the act to obtain drugs. Therefore your affiant wishes to seize known body fluids, to wit: blood and urine for the purpose of drug screening from Miller and Solomon.

Your affiant knows from past experience that private and law enforcement laboratories (FBI and Maryland State Police) can perform specific scientific tests to obtain blood type and DNA results. Your affiant also knows the laboratories can identify the origin of hair fibers when comparing known and recovered samples. The laboratories can also do toxicology screening of known body fluids to determine if certain drugs are present in the fluids."

The application was taken to the Honorable Russel Sadler, Judge of the District Court for Howard County who reviewed the facts before him. Upon determining there were sufficient grounds for the issuance of a Search and Seizure Warrant, Judge Sadler commanded the warrant be executed and evidence pertaining to the case seized.

Rodney Solomon and Bernard Miller were released from the Howard County Detention Center on a Writ of Habeas Corpus and taken to Howard County General Hospital where appropriate samples were seized in the presence of Detective First Class Thomas Martin.

***

Sergeant Michael Fischer of the Maryland State Police, an expert in the field of accident reconstruction, was called to assist in the investigation.

Sergeant Fischer said, "I had the opportunity to view several photographs taken of the deceased by the medical examiner's office. One photograph of primary importance to me was of the deceased in a supine position on an examining table with her left arm upright, fully extended.

This photograph reveals several items of importance relative to the investigation. First, there is an impression on the left upper arm midway between the elbow and shoulder, which clearly shows the imprint of the tongue and plastic support of the seatbelt. The tongue position is upward from the rear of the body towards the front. The belt is wrapped in a counter-clockwise direction around the left upper arm two (2) half turns and one complete turn for a total of two (2) revolutions. Its beginning is at the aforementioned tongue and the marks conclude where the webbing is against the left upper arm by the front portion of the shoulder.

Utilizing the above listed photograph a computer-digitized image was reproduced via Hewlett Packard Scan-Jet Plus. The computer was programmed to separate the thickness layers of the victim's arm in the area of the belt damage. This image indicates the depth of the intrusion from the seatbelt and its tongue into the victim's body tissue. The deepest intrusion into the body tissue is indicated by the darkest shade, while the lightest areas indicate little or no tissue intrusion. With this fact the digitized image indicated deepest tissue involvement in the area of the tongue, the first complete wrap of the seatbelt and the shoulder area.

The next area of interest is on the bottom portion of the victim's left arm. This is an incised type wound in an "L" configuration in the soft flabby tissue. It appears from its shape and character that the victim's arm was caught in the bottom portion of the door jam at the rear of the left front (driver's) door. These wounds are noted on the digital image.

There are significant stretch marks, specifically in the area of the left armpit, rotating forward towards the shoulder area. From the shoulder area these marks transverse downward to and through the complete wrap of the seatbelt. The characteristics of these stretch marks appear that the body was pulled with the head towards the front of the vehicle and the feet towards the rear. The left shoulder was in a slightly elevated position.

I had the opportunity to examine a 1990 BMW 4S, bearing Maryland Registration WMN 492, the vehicle involved in Mrs. Basu's death.

A complete photographing of the seatbelt and mechanisms from the rest to fully extracted positions was completed, which included front and back sides. Several marks of interest on the belt were also photographed. These marks include rubs along portions of the belt, crimping of the belt webbing, and what appeared to be body fluid stains on the webbing. Along the floorboard at the left side of the driver's seat, on a plastic appearing panel, were numerous scrapes, abrasions and rub marks. On the rear of the jam on left front driver's door were scrapes, abrasions and rub marks in the painted metal surface. Most of the paint in this area was rubbed off exposing the bare metal. This mark is of the type that a material would have caused the paint deformation/destruction. There were no corresponding marks on the door itself or any door components where it connected to the door jam. It appears that the seatbelt was extracted into the lower portion of the door making contact with the plastic appearing panel and painted door jam surface, causing corresponding marks on these items and the belt webbing.

There were fold marks on the belt, which when extracted correspond to those marks on the victim's body. Maryland State Police Crime Lab personnel took a blood presence test on the belt in this area of concern. Additionally, information was requested as to the extent of the blood travel on the belt webbing in this area. These results will be forwarded in another report. Preliminarily, however, the test was positive for human blood.

In conclusion, it is my opinion that Mrs. Pam Basu became entangled in the left front (driver's) seatbelt webbing of this 1990 BMW 4S, from and through the front door. As the victim fell to the ground, physical evidence indicated her initial position was feet forward. The body then began to rotate and bounce, at which time the seatbelt webbing became further entangled around her left arm with one complete wrap holding the tongue firmly against her left arm. The body continued to bounce and was dragged in a position with the victim's head forward towards the front of the car and the feet towards the rear of the car. It also appears that her left leg may have been folded or bent at the knee. Mrs. Basu's left arm also appears to have been caught at the bottom rear of the driver's door, as evidenced by the size, nature and type of wound on the left upper arm soft tissue. Mrs. Basu's left side was elevated from the restricted movement of the seatbelt and arm in the door. The position of the body at this time was face/belly down towards the road surface. The intensity of the tissue invasion from the computer generation and for purposes of the seatbelt evaluation to the left arm appears to be deepest at the points where the tongue touched the left upper arm and finally near the top of the left upper arm at the shoulder."

Test results on other evidence obtained during the course of the investigation will be forthcoming.

Thirteen

On Thursday, September 10, 1992 at about 10:53 AM Detective First Class Tom Martin received a collect telephone call from Bernard Eric Miller. Miller asked Martin when detectives would return to talk with him and told Martin that he was hiring an attorney. When asked by Martin if he still wished to speak with detectives he said, "Yes."

At about 1:10 PM Miller was taken from the Howard County Detention Center per a writ of Habeas Corpus and driven to Howard County Police Headquarters to be interviewed. Detective Lee Lachman would again talk with Miller in the presence of Detective First Class Martin. What follows are excerpts from that interview.

    Lachman: Now, Bernard just to go over a couple of things real quick. This morning, while you were at the detention center, you asked somebody to call me, is that correct?

    Miller: Yes.

    Lachman: Okay, and why did you want them to call me?

    Miller: Because I wanted to tell the truth.

Lachman:	And you asked me to come down and talk to you, is that right?
Miller:	Yes.
Lachman:	And you know that you have the right to have a lawyer here with you and we've advised you of your rights, and you want to talk to us without a lawyer, is that right?
Miller:	Yes.
Lachman:	Where'd you go when you got to the rest area?
Miller:	A vending machine.
Lachman:	Did you get anything out of there?
Miller:	Yes.
Lachman:	What did you get?
Miller:	Some potato chips.
Lachman:	Okay, then what happened? Did Rodney do anything?
Miller:	He tried to put a dollar in there to get change so he could use the phone.
Lachman:	Okay, he tried to call somebody?
Miller:	Yes.
Lachman:	And did he get a hold of them?
Miller:	No.
Lachman:	Then what happened?
Miller:	Rodney said we was gonna get another car.
Lachman:	And did he say how to get the car?
Miller:	He was gonna rough somebody's car off.
Lachman:	And what's that mean?
Miller:	Forcefully take somebody's car.
Lachman:	Then what happened?
Miller:	Then we walked over to a man standing—sitting in his car drinking coffee. Rodney tried to take the man up out his car. The man called for help.

Lachman:	Did you grab the man?
Miller:	Yes.
Lachman:	Okay, where did he grab him?
Miller:	He grabbed his arm out the car. The man hollered for help.
Lachman:	Uh huh.
Miller:	I was standin' waitin' for Rodney, lookin' around waitin' for the police.
Lachman:	Uh huh.
Miller:	Then that's when we saw another lady at the car.
Lachman:	Okay.
Miller:	Rodney say he's gonna take her keys forcefully.
Lachman:	Uh huh.
Miller:	He—he… The lady hollered for help. Then that's when me and Rodney took off runnin'. We ran through some townhouses.
Lachman:	Okay.
Miller:	Then that's when we saw the lady standin' at the Caravan. She was walkin' up to the door.
Lachman:	Did she have any kids with her or anything?
Miller:	She had a kid in the car and was walkin' up to the house to get another kid.
Lachman:	Did Rodney go up to her?
Miller:	Rodney went up to her to ask her could he use her phone. The lady said no. Rodney stood by her Caravan waitin' for the lady to come back down, right. I was standin' around on the sidewalk. The lady said no. Rodney snatched her keys. The lady hollered—hollered for help and said I can identify you. I can identify you. Rodney

	took off runnin'. Me and Rodney started joggin' down the street passed some school kids. We saw a man standin' with an umbrella drinkin' coffee.
Lachman:	Uh huh.
Miller:	So we ran up the street. Ran through some townhouses. We spotted a Brown BMW where a lady was loadin' her baby in the car seat.
Lachman:	Okay, so you all saw her loading the baby in the car seat?
Miller:	Yes. Then me and Rodney waited for the lady at the stop sign.
Lachman:	When you were waiting for her at the stop sign, did you all talk about anything?
Miller:	He just said he was gonna rough her off. He said this time we gonna get this car. He said this is the only car we could get.
Lachman:	And what did he tell you to do?
Miller:	He told me that he was gonna take the lady out the car and I was gonna drive.
Lachman:	You're talking about Rodney telling you this?
Miller:	Yes, yes.
Lachman:	So the lady came up to the stop sign. Then what did you all do?
Miller:	Rodney opened the car door.
Lachman:	Uh huh.
Miller:	The lady looked at Rodney. Rodney forcefully grabbed the lady by her neck. I got in the car, started the car up, put the car in drive. Rodney walked around to the passenger side. Rodney got in the passenger side?

Lachman:	When Rodney walked up to the car, did he say anything to the lady when she was stopped at the Stop sign?
Miller:	He said get out.
Lachman:	Did he open her door?
Miller:	Yes.
Lachman:	He opened the driver's side door?
Miller:	Yes.
Lachman:	When he grabbed her, what did he say to her?
Miller:	He said get out the damn car.
Lachman:	Did he grab her by the throat or neck?
Miller:	He grabbed her by the throat.
Lachman:	He pulled her out of the car. Now, when she came out of the car, what happened to her?
Miller:	She was hooked to the seatbelt.
Lachman:	Which arm?
Miller:	Left arm.
Lachman:	Was she struggling with Rodney?
Miller:	She was strugglin' with Rodney.
Lachman:	Was she saying anything?
Miller:	No, she was just shocked.
Lachman:	And while Rodney was struggling with her, while her arm was caught in the seatbelt, that's when you got into the driver's seat?
Miller:	Yes.
Lachman:	Did you close the driver's door?
Miller:	Yes.
Lachman:	What happened when you closed the driver's door?
Miller:	I put the car in drive. Rodney ran around to the passenger's side. He set in the car. I pulled off.

Lachman:	When you closed the door, what was she doing outside the car?
Miller:	Draggin'.
Lachman:	When you first closed the door, what was she doing while the car was still?
Miller:	She wasn't doin' nothin'. She was just layin' down. Her head face down, butt up.
Lachman:	Rodney got in the passenger's seat and closed the door. What was the baby doing then?
Miller:	Hollerin' in the backseat. Makin' a loud aggravatin' noise.
Lachman:	So, you pulled off and the lady was dragging, then what happened?
Miller:	I drove the car for about a mile draggin' the lady. Rodney was on the passenger side. Then we took the baby out the backseat.
Lachman:	Now, when you went to take the baby out of the backseat, why'd you take the baby out?
Miller:	Because it was makin' loud aggravatin' noises.
Lachman:	Okay, did you pull the car off the side of the road?
Miller:	Yes.
Lachman:	And did you get out the driver's door?
Miller:	Yes.
Lachman:	When you got out the driver's door, did you walk around the front of the car and go to the rear passenger side door?
Miller:	Yes.
Lachman:	What did you do once you opened the door?
Miller:	Rodney unhooked the seatbelt. I tossed the baby out the car.

Lachman:	Explain how you tossed the baby out of the car.
Miller:	I threw the baby out.
Lachman:	Did you throw it out in the seat—in the car seat?
Miller:	Yes.
Lachman:	When you threw the baby out, did you throw it on the ground?
Miller:	Yes.
Lachman:	When you stopped the car to take the baby out, did you have a hard time getting the door open?
Miller:	Yes.
Lachman:	What did you have to do to get the door open?
Miller:	I kicked the door open.
Lachman:	Did you have a hard time getting the door open because the lady's body was in the way?
Miller:	Yes.
Lachman:	And when you got out of the car, did you brush up against the lady?
Miller:	Yes.
Lachman:	Did you get blood on you?
Miller:	Yes.

Miller at this time spoke of driving away while continuing to drag the victim's body along Gorman Road, losing control of the car and striking the fence.

Lachman:	What happened when you hit the barbed wire fence? Did you open the door?
Miller:	I opened the car door up.
Lachman:	What did you see?
Miller:	I saw the body.
Lachman:	And what did it look like?

Miller:	It looked fleshy. Bloody.
Lachman:	Was there any clothes on the woman?
Miller:	No.
Lachman:	Did you see her head?
Miller:	I seen her head.
Lachman:	What did her head look like?
Miller:	It looked bloody.
Lachman:	And what did the rest of her body look like?
Miller:	Scarred up white flesh.
Lachman:	The flesh was messed up?
Miller:	Yes.
Lachman:	Once you saw the body, did you close the driver's door?
Miller:	I closed the door.

Miller said he backed up and drove away still dragging the woman. He stopped the car because Rodney said he was going to drive.

Lachman:	Okay, you stopped the car. Then what happened?
Miller:	Rodney got out the passenger side. He unhooked the lady off the seatbelt. He snatched the lady. Unhooked her left arm from the seatbelt.
Lachman:	So, he tore the seatbelt off her arm?
Miller:	Yes.
Lachman:	And how did you get out of the car?
Miller:	I got out the driver's side.
Lachman:	Did you brush up against her then?
Miller:	I brushed up against her.
Lachman:	And got more blood on you?
Miller:	Yes.
Lachman:	Then what did you do?

Miller: I walked to the passenger's side and Rodney began to drive because he said he looked older.

Miller once again told Lachman how they drove away from the body and began throwing his clothing out of the car because it was stained with Pam Basu's blood. He also told Lachman how they drove to the car wash to wash away the blood and to get rid of Pam Basu's personal belongings. His story continued, detailing their flight and their arrest by police after they left the car wash.

Lachman: Now, is this the whole truth about what happened?
Miller: Yes.
Lachman: Now we've had two—three conversations and this is the final conversation we're having and this is now the truth, right?
Miller: Yes.
Lachman: And you're just telling me the truth now because you want to get it all out in the open and you want to make sure the truth is known?
Miller: Yes.

The interview concluded at about 1:52 PM on September 10, 1992.

Detective First Class Martin and Detective Lachman would later document the many discrepancies in Miller's stories. They believed his stories might have changed because of death threats made to him by Rodney Solomon. During Bernard Eric Miller's first statement, which was not taped, he told Lachman that Rodney said, "We partners in crime. If you tell anybody, I'll kill you."

To add substance to the possibility of additional threats DFC Martin learned through an interview with a corrections officer that Solomon was able to communicate with Miller. Although the two were housed some distance apart in separate isolation cells, verbal exchanges were made via the vents of the heating and air conditioning ducts.

Fatal Destiny

Fourteen

Detective First Class Tom Martin requested laboratory tests be conducted on evidence recovered during the investigation and that seized from Solomon and Miller. The National Center of Forensic Science, 1901 Sulphur Spring Road, Baltimore, Maryland performed tests to determined if there were drugs in the system of Solomon and Miller. The results of those tests were returned to prosecutors and police and disclosed data on each of the suspects.

Miller, Bernard:

The urine specimen was screened by enzyme immunoassay with the following results:

Amphetamines	Negative
Barbiturate	Negative
Benzodiazepines	Negative
Cannabinoids (Marijuana)	**Positive**
Cocaine (Metabolite)	Negative
Methadone	Negative
Opiates	Negative
Phencyclidine (PCP)	**Positive**
Propoxyphene	Negative

The drugs in the urine, which screened positive above, were confirmed by gas chromatography mass spectrometry as follows:

    Phencyclidine (PCP) **Positive** 630 ng/ml

    11-nor-delta-9-tetrahydro-Cannabinol-9-carboxylic acid **Positive** 6 ng/ml

Solomon, Rodney E.:

Amphetamines	Negative
Barbiturates	Negative
Benzodiazepines	Negative
Cannabinoids (Marijuana)	**Positive**
Cocaine (Metabolite)	**Positive**
Methadone	Negative
Opiates	Negative
Phencyclidine (PCP)	**Positive**
Propoxyphene	Negative

The drugs in the urine which screen positive above were confirmed by gas chromatography mass spectrometry as follows:

    Phencyclidine **Positive** 560 ng/ml

    11-nor-delata-9-tetrahydro-Cannabinol-9-carboxylic acid **Positive** 8 ng/ml

    Cocaine (Metabolite) **Positive** 120 ng/ml

The Maryland State Police Crime Laboratory also conducted tests on evidence submitted and returned their findings to Detective First Class Tom Martin.

Results of Examination/Analysis:

    01:    Black Jordache knee length shorts. Stains on this item were tested for the presence of blood with negative results.

02: Black/Purple Peach Pipe Line Swimming Trunks. Stains on this item were tested for the presence of blood with negative results.

03: Black Salem Sportswear XL T-shirt with Washington Redskins Emblem. Stains on this item were tested for the presence of blood with negative results.

04: Pair of Black and White Stripes Adidas High Top Sneakers. Stains on both sneakers were tested for the presence of blood with negative results.

05: Pair of white ankle high socks. Stains on this item were tested for the presence of blood with negative results.

06: White T-shirt "TJ" Stains on this item were tested for the presence of blood with negative results.

07: Hairs removed from shirt. Several hairs were found in this item.

08: Black and White Jacket from suspect Miller. Human blood was identified in a portion of the bloodstains found on the left collar area of this item. PGM(IEF): 1+2-enzyme type was identified.

09: Black Adidas Tennis Shoes from suspect Miller. Human blood was identified in a portion of the bloodstains found on the right shoe. PGM(IEF): 1+2-enzyme type was identified. Human blood was identified in a portion of the bloodstains found on the left shoe. PGM(IEF): 1+2-enzyme type was identified.

10: One (1) pair of black socks from suspect Miller .Blood was indicated in a portion of the stains found on this item. Origin determination was inconclusive.

11: One (1) pair of white shorts/red stripes from suspect Miller. Human blood was identified in a portion of

the bloodstains found on the front of this item.
Enzyme typing tests were inconclusive.

12: Body debris and hair. Human blood was identified in a portion of the stains found on this item. PGM(IEF): 1+ enzyme type was identified.
One (1) hair was found in this item.

13: Blood swab from roof of 1990 BMW.
Human blood was identified in a portion of the stains found on this item.
PGM(IEF): 1+ enzyme type was identified.

14: Blood swab from dashboard of 1990 BMW. Human blood was identified in a portion of the bloodstains found on this item. PGM(IEF): 1+ enzyme type was identified.

15: Plastic floor mat with possible blood from left front floor. Human blood was identified in a portion of the bloodstains found on this item. PGM(IEF): 1+ enzyme type was identified.

16: Plastic floor mat with possible blood from right front floor. Human blood was identified in a portion of the bloodstains found on this item. PGM(IEF): 1+ enzyme was identified.

17: Carpeted floor mat with possible blood from left front floor. Stains on this item were tested for the presence of blood with negative results.

18: Carpeted floor mat with possible blood from right front floor. Human blood was identified in a portion of the bloodstains found on this item. PGM(IEF): 1+ enzyme type was identified.

19: BMW hubcap from left rear wheel. Human blood was identified in a portion of the bloodstains found on this item. Enzyme typing tests were inconclusive.

20: Hair from around left rear wheel axle.

21: Blood/body tissue from left rear wheel well.
Human blood was identified in a portion of the stains found on this item. PGM(IEF): 1+ enzyme type was identified.

22: Navy blue jogging pants.
Human blood was identified in a portion of the bloodstains found on this item. PGM(IEF): 1+ enzyme type was identified.

23: Bloodstained pink slacks.
Human blood was identified in a portion of the bloodstains on this item.
PGM(IEF): 1+ enzyme was identified.
Material was missing from the right front area of this item.

24: Bloodstained panties
Human blood was identified in a portion of the bloodstains found on this item. PFM(IEF): 1+ enzyme was identified.
Material was separated along the waist area of this item.

25: Skull tissue from bent pole.
Human blood was identified in a portion of the bloodstains found on this item. PGM(IEF): 1+ enzyme type was identified.

26: Tissue from bent pole.
Human blood was identified in a portion of the bloodstains found on this item. PGM(IEF): 1+ enzyme type was identified.

27: Tissue fragment from grass behind pole.
Human blood was identified in a portion of the bloodstains found on this item. Enzyme typing tests were inconclusive.

28: Tissue fragment from grass behind wire fence.

Human blood was identified in a portion of the bloodstains found on this item. Enzyme typing tests were inconclusive.

29: Tissue fragment from wire fence.
Human blood was identified in a portion of the bloodstains found on this item. Enzyme typing tests were inconclusive.

30: Tissue fragment from wooden stake.
Human blood was identified in a portion of the bloodstains found on this item. Enzyme typing tests were inconclusive.

31: Vial of blood from victim – Basu.
The following genetic markers were identified in a portion of the whole blood sample of Pam Basu:

ABO:	Group B
Lewis:	le a-b- (Inconclusive secretor status)
PGM(IEF):	1+
EAP(IEF):	B
ADA:	1
AK:	1
CAII:	1
PepA:	1

32: Hair combing (Basu)
33: Rib sample (Basu)
34: Spleen sample (Basu)
35: Muscle sample (Basu)
36: Vial of blood from suspect – Miller
The following genetic markers were identified in the whole blood sample of Bernard Miller:

ABO:	Group B
Lewis:	Le a-b+ Secretor
PGM(IEF):	1+2-
EAP(IEF):	B

	ADA:	1
	AK:	1
	CAII:	1
	PepA:	1

37: Vial of blood from suspect – Solomon.
The following genetic markers were identified in the whole blood sample of Rodney Solomon:

ABO:	Group B
Lewis:	Le a-b- (Inconclusive Secretor status)
PGM(IEF):	1-2+
EAP(IEF):	B
ADA:	1
AK:	1
CAII:	1
PepA:	1

38: Victim's left shoe.
Stains on this item were tested for the presence of blood with negative results.

39: Victim's right shoe.
Stains on this item were tested for the presence of blood with negative results.

A second report was submitted to DFC Martin from the Maryland State Police Crime Laboratory regarding other tests conducted.

01: Scrapings from T-shirt
The following were noted in this item:
1) Soil
2) Vegetable matter
3) Several small hairs and fragments (not suitable for comparison purposes)
4) Debris

02: Hairs removed from with T-shirt

Several small hairs and fragments (not suitable for comparison purposes) and one blue/gray dyed animal hair were noted in this item.

- 03: Known head hair sample from victim
- 04: Known head hair sample from Miller
- 05: Known head hair sample from Solomon
- 06: Scrapings from socks
  The following were noted in this item:
  1) Soil
  2) Vegetable matter
  3) Several Negroid hairs and fragments
  4) Numerous small hairs and fragments (not suitable for comparison purposes)
  5) One Caucasian pubic hair
  6) Lint
  7) Debris
- 07: Scrapings from high top sneakers
  The following were noted in this item:
  1) Soil
  2) Vegetable matter
  3) Several hair fragments (not suitable for comparison purposes)
  4) Debris
- 08: Scrapings from socks
  Two pubic hair fragments were noted in this item.
- 09: Scrapings from jogging trousers
  The following noted in this item:
  1) Vegetable matter
  2) Numerous Negroid hairs and fragments
  3) One Caucasian head hair fragment (not suitable for comparison purposes)
- 10: Scrapings from driver's seat belt

One head hair consistent in color and morphology with the known head hair of the victim was noted in this item.

11: Scrapings from left front floor mat
The following were noted in this item:
1) Soil
2) Vegetable matter
3) Debris

12: Scrapings from left front floor mat
The following were noted in this item:
1) Soil
2) Vegetable matter
3) Lint
4) Numerous head hairs consistent in color and morphology with known head hairs of the victim.
5) Numerous hairs and fragments (not suitable for comparison purposes)
6) Debris

13: Scrapings from right front floor mat
The following were noted in this item:
1) Soil
2) Vegetable matter
3) Lint
4) Several head hairs consistent in color and morphology with the known head hair of the victim.
5) Numerous hairs and fragments (not suitable for comparison purposes)
6) Debris

14: Hair samples from rear axle
Numerous head hairs consistent in color and morphology with the known head hair of the victim were noted in this item.

Conclusion:

Head hairs consistent in color and morphology with the known head hair of the victim were noted in the scrapings from the driver's seatbelt, scrapings from the left front floor mat, scrapings from the from the right front floor mat and from the rear axle.

From the information provided by the Maryland State Police Crime Laboratory, poster sized charts would be prepared for use in presenting the facts and evidence to the jury at the time of trial.

Fifteen

While preparations for the prosecution and defense of Solomon and Miller were moving forward, Rodney Solomon believed he could not receive a fair trial in Howard County. Despite objections from his attorney, Carol Hanson of the Howard County Public Defender's Office, he filed a motion for and was granted a change of venue. His case would be tried in the Baltimore County Circuit Court in August 1993. Bernard Eric Miller's trial was scheduled to begin Monday, April 12, 1993 in Howard County before Circuit Court Judge, The Honorable Dennis M. Sweeney and a panel of jurors.

As the trial date moved closer, the Howard County Sheriff's Office was charged with the responsibility of providing personal safety and security during the trial of Bernard Miller. Sheriff Michael Chiuchiolo carefully planned his strategy for the trial and the sure to be onslaught of media and private citizens to the Howard County Court House. His operational plan ensured a high visibility of uniformed Sheriff's Deputies both inside and on the outer perimeter of the historic court building. He hired additional temporary deputies and assigned them to work in plain clothes within the confines of the courtroom for added security. He appointed Deputy Sheriff Randolph Roby to act as his liaison officer and to provide members of the news media with daily information regarding the trial. He reserved three rows of benches in the courtroom for the press corps, artists and television commentators. In addition, he provided for them a pressroom complete with telephones, in the basement of the courthouse. Members of the press would later compliment Sheriff Chiuchiolo and his staff, stating they could not recall ever having been treated with such professional courtesy.

From the Howard County State's Attorneys Office, Michael Rexrode, Joseph Murtha and Christine Gage would undertake the difficult task of preparing and prosecuting the cases. Late nights and working weekends would be the order of business for the trio of prosecutors.

In the initial stages of the preparations Rodney Solomon was informed of the State's intention to seek the death penalty for his part in the crime. Because of Bernard Miller's age at the time of the crime they could not ask for the death penalty in his case.

As the trial opened on April 12, 1993 Senior Assistant State's Attorney Michael Rexrode stood, faced the jury and delivered his opening statement. The following is an excerpt from that statement.

"This was a very special day for Dr. Pam and Steve Basu. A very special day, as this was the day when the joy of their life, Sarina, was to start preschool. Pam Basu had been planning for, if not months for this day. It was a very special day for them and they were getting ready. And, as they were getting Sarina ready, Steve Basu got his video camera out to memorialize the event. He took some pictures inside the home that morning as she's getting ready for her first day at school, then goes out front and videotapes Sarina and Pam as they're walking out to their car parked right in front of their home.

Pam Basu and Sarina are videotaped and they're waving to dad as he's videotaping, like many of us might do if we're fortunate enough to have a video camera. And in the background of that videotape we see those two strangers to the neighborhood—Bernard Eric Miller and Rodney Solomon, captured on Steve Basu's videotape as they walked by. As they waved goodbye for the final time Pam got into her car and put her child in the backseat where Sarina's car seat was kept.

The plan that morning was that Pam was going to take Sarina, and Steve was going to follow and they were going to take some more videotape at the school when they got there. Steve was going to drive a different car so they could go to work following Sarina's first day at school and after they met all of the school officials. Pam left as Steve was going back into the house to finish getting his video and other equipment ready. The car came to a Stop Sign at Knights Bridge Road. Pam, being very careful, looked both ways. And at this point, as she looked both ways, she was accosted first by Rodney Solomon. She was grabbed. She was attacked. She was hit. She was slugged through the window of her car. And, as Rodney Solomon attacked her, Bernard Eric Miller ran up to join in the fray, to join in the attack on Pam Basu. Bernard Eric Miller jumps in the car, in the passenger seat while Rodney Solomon is attacking from the driver's seat, trying to pull Pam from her automobile. And with the help of both of them, especially with the help of Bernard Eric Miller inside Pam's car—kicking and pushing and shoving on one side by Bernard Eric Miller in the passenger's seat, and Rodney Solomon pulling from the driver's side, with the door now open, Pam Basu is forced to the ground outside her car. She's fighting, she's screaming. Her child is still in the car. She jumps up, goes back to the window to reach for her child. The door is slammed shut and the two attempt to make their getaway. But the seatbelt is wrapped around Pam Basu's arm and she's running with the car. She's heard to say **'my baby! My baby!'** as she's running with the car. As she's fighting for her child in the car, the car speeds up, accelerates fast, and she falls.

A shoe is left at the intersection. She can't hold her—keep up with the car and, as she falls, her head smashes to the ground and she begins tumbling and she begins being dragged by this car all the way to the Stop Sign where Horsham Drive comes to Gorman Road. She's still being dragged and as the car pulls out from this intersection it pulls over and stops.

Why does it stop? Because there's a child in the car. Do they set the child down? Do they take it to a home? Do they give it care? **No!** They grabbed Sarina, like they could care less for her life, grabbed her and threw her to the ground near the road. And then they take off, rapidly accelerating and speeding down this road, sometimes fifty, sixty miles an hour. Right in front of the elementary school, right in front of the friends and neighbors of Steve and Pam Basu who were taking their kids to school. And then there was a curve in the road, a marked curve with a fence of barbed wire, and they went and skimmed that fence to pull Pam Basu from the side of the car, wrapping her in barbed wire. They didn't stop. They went further down the road and at this point—one point seven miles later, they remove Pam Basu from the car. Do they have the dignity to place her to the side of the road? **No!** They leave her in the middle of the road, wrapped in barbed wire with a trail of her body that can literally be walked and tracked back to the point of the attack.

Where do they go from here? Well, we know where they went. And as they went along their way they threw items out of the car at different points. A driver's license here, at the intersection of 216 and 29, a shoe. Down at the intersection of Pindell School Road and 216, a briefcase. Then over where Highland Road is, another briefcase. From here they went all the way to Eldersburg and with a Paltry $6.95 they went to a car wash to wash the blood of Pam Basu, the evidence of the crime, from her automobile. From there, and that is where law enforcement was fortunate, they virtually reversed their course and came back down into Howard County.

They came down to Route 108 and it just happened that the police had a roadblock set up at the intersection of Route 108 and 216 in Highland, Maryland. A quiet little place called Highland Junction. And sure enough, as they're going this way, they're spotted by a Maryland State Trooper. He gives chase. He chases them right into the roadblock. If you know the place, there's a place called Boarman's Store at the inter-section of Highland Junction, and there they had the roadblock set up. As they slammed on their brakes for the roadblock, they threw the car into reverse and bailed out right here a mile from Highland Junction.

Rodney Solomon was the first to get out because he had the clearest escape from the vehicle. As he backed up he lost control and went off the road and had the clearest route of escape. But Bernard Eric Miller didn't have such a sure way of exit because he was in the middle of thorns and bushes. Police were in the chase. Bernard Eric Miller was captured on Pam Basu's BMW as he tried to climb across the hood to get away. Rodney Solomon tried to make an escape and was caught with the help of a Maryland State Police Medivac Helicopter, which landed and the medic ran and captured Rodney Solomon.

Ladies and Gentlemen, during the course of the trial you will hear from eyewitnesses. From eyewitnesses who were at the intersection when Pam Basu was attacked at the Stop sign. You will hear from two separate eyewitnesses who observed the attack, who observed the defendant in Pam Basu's car attacking her. You will hear from eye-witnesses who observed Sarina being thrown to the ground. You will hear from witnesses, from mothers and fathers in this area of the school who observed Bernard Eric Miller and Rodney Solomon in their neighborhood. And, Ladies and Gentlemen, you will hear from Steve Basu. He will tell you about that day in his life. He will tell you about how he made the videotape, which you will see during the course of this trial. And, when you look at the videotape you will see the defendant on videotape as he walked in front of the Basu residence.

You will hear from various experts, experts on hairs and fibers and serology. Serology is the study of blood and an expert on serology will tell you that this defendant has the blood of Pam Basu on his clothing, on his shoes and on his pants. You will hear from the Medical Examiner who will tell you of the last day and minutes of Pam Basu's life. How she was literally pulled and dragged until the life was dragged out of her. He will tell you the condition of her body and the horrible, horrible injuries she sustained until her body, wrapped with barbed wire, was finally removed from the car.

You will hear from fingerprint experts, persons whose occupational specialty and expertise is the comparison of fingerprints. They will tell you that the fingerprints of Rodney Solomon and this defendant were found inside Pam Basu's vehicle. That the fingerprints of Bernard Eric Miller were found on Pam Basu's credit cards as well as inside the car.

Finally, you will see the clothing that's been recovered from the defendants. Bernard Miller's white shirt, which was thrown from the car as he's making his escape. Bernard Miller's pants, which he actually took off and threw out of the car as he's making his escape. For when Bernard Miller was arrested as he climbed over the hood of Pam Basu's vehicle he only had on his boxer shorts, athletic style jacket and his shoes. He had, with that guilty knowledge, discarded his clothing. And you will see the clothing of Rodney Solomon, the black Redskin sweatshirt and the black shorts he had on.

Ladies and Gentlemen, at the conclusion of the trial I will have the opportunity to speak to you again. During that opportunity, I will predict right now in preview of which I will ask you... I will ask you, based upon all the evidence that has been presented in this case—the diagrams, the charts, the videotape, the witnesses, the documentary evidence, the experts, and the eyewitnesses who have testified from this stand... I will ask you to find Bernard Eric Miller guilty of the robbery and attempted theft from Grace Lagana, of the assault with the intent to rob Laura Becraft, of the murder, the robbery and kidnapping of Dr. Pam Basu and the kidnapping of Sarina Basu.

I thank you very much for your attention."

With opening statements completed the first witness was called to the stand. And, one by one, a steady stream of witnesses walked to the front of the courtroom and painted for the jury a grisly tale of what they saw on a bright, beautiful sunlit Tuesday morning in September. When asked if they could identify the man responsible for what they had described in their testimony their heads turned toward the defense table, arms raised and fingers pointed directly to Bernard Eric Miller.

At one point during the testimony when a witness gave a very vivid description of how she saw the body being dragged beside the car, Miller looked over his shoulder at members of his family and friends, seated in the courtroom, and smiled.

The experts too were called to the stand to tell the jury of their findings. They told of Bernard Eric Miller's fingerprints being found on Pam Basu's 1990 BMW and on her credit cards. Another told of how blood found on Miller's clothing matched the genetic markers of Pam Basu's blood. Still another testified that the car's striking of the fence on Gorman Road was an intentional act.

Steve Basu took the stand and, sometimes with a trembling voice, told the jury of joyfully seeing Pam and Sarina off for their daughter's fist day of preschool. As his story reached a critical point his voice cracked and he began to weep. Family and friends cried openly in the courtroom. Many of those who filled the courtroom merely as curious observers, some members of the jury and a number in the press corps lowered their heads and wiped at the tears filling their eyes. When some minutes passed and Steve Basu regained his composure, he completed his story of a day with a joyous beginning and a sad, tragic ending.

Officer Jody Tookey was asked to take the witness stand and tell the jury about her finding of the body of Pam Basu on Gorman Road. At this point in the trial State's Attorney Michael Rexrode produced a poster-sized piece of brown wrapping paper and carried it to the front of the witness stand. As he peeled back the paper to reveal a photograph to Officer Tookey, Judge Dennis Sweeney leaned forward in his chair to look at the picture. His eyes opened wide as he caught a glimpse of the first photograph. A few moments later State's Attorney Rexrode unveiled a second photograph of the victim. As Judge Sweeney looked at the second picture his eyes again widened and he turned away.

The prosecution would introduce only two photographs of the victim and those were showing her just as she was discovered, face down in the roadway. Mr. Rexrode believed the remaining photographs to be far too brutal and inflammatory to show to the jury.

After Officer Tookey identified the photographs and they were introduced into evidence, Judge Sweeney called a recess in the proceedings.

It was early afternoon when court reconvened and Michael Rexrode stepped to the front of the jurors to give them their first view of the photographs. When Mr. Rexrode held up the first picture in front of them, some gasped, a few quickly lowered their heads, a man seated in the first row of jurors stared in disbelief as he complexion turned chalk white and a woman wept as the picture passed in front of her.

Judge Sweeney would later permit members of the press and court artists to view the photographs. He did, however, sternly warm them against depicting the scene portrayed in the pictures.

Assistant State's Attorney Joseph Murtha thought he would call Tony Angelo Williams, one of the passengers in the Cadillac on September 8, 1992, as a witness for the prosecution. Williams, accompanied by his father, arrived at the courthouse in response to his summons to testify. Mr. Murtha, still undecided about calling

Williams to the stand tried to speak with him outside the courtroom. At that time Williams' father became belligerent and loudly informed Mr. Murtha he didn't want his son testifying for the prosecution. Mr. Murtha said, "He got right up in my face and told me his son was a defense witness."

Bernard Miller's defense attorney, Laurack Bray, objected to Mr. Murtha's attempt to speak with Williams stating he was interfering with his witness. Rather than create further controversy Mr. Murtha declined to call Tony Williams to the stand.

On Thursday afternoon, April 22, 1993 the case was turned over to the jury for deliberation. As Sheriff's Deputies escorted Bernard Eric Miller from the courtroom to await their findings he smiled and said, "I be walkin' soon."

When asked by one of the deputies what he meant, he said, "They gonna find me not guilty. I'm goin' home."

The jury deliberated well into the night before breaking for a few hours rest. They returned to the deliberation room before noon on Friday, April 23rd to complete their duties. When word was sent out that they had reached a verdict in the case, the news spread quickly throughout the courthouse. In a matter of minutes Mrs. Basu's family and friends filed into the courtroom and sat huddled together in the back of the room. And moments later, artists, reporters, television commentators, clerks and secretaries filled the courtroom to capacity.

Judge Dennis Sweeney took his place on the bench and although the room was silent, the air was charged with anxious anticipation. Eyes were fixed on the doorway to the deliberation room and it seemed as though the entire assembly held its collective breath. At last the door opened, jurors appeared one by one and walked in silence to their chairs in the jury box. When the last member was seated the Foreman of the Jury stood to answer the questions that filled the minds of everyone in the room.

On the charge of robbery of the keys to a Chrysler automobile from Grace Lagana, do you find the defendant not guilty or guilty?

Not Guilty. (With that announcement, Miller grinned, guessing that he was going to walk out a free man.)

On the charge of the assault of Grace Lagana, do you find the defendant not guilty or guilty?

Guilty.

On the charge of the battery of Grace Lagana, do you find the defendant not guilty or guilty?

Guilty.

On the charge of the attempted theft of the Chrysler automobile from Grace Lagana, do you find the defendant not guilty or guilty?

Guilty.

On the charge of the assault with the intent to rob Laura Ann Becraft of her automobile, do you find the defendant not guilty or guilty?

Guilty.

On the charge of the robbery of the BMW automobile from Pam Basu, do you find the defendant not guilty or guilty?

Guilty.

On the charge of felony murder of Pam Basu, do you find the defendant not guilty or guilty?

Guilty.

With that announcement, there were sighs and tears from the Basu family. Pam Basu's father lowered his head and through the tears it looked as though he whispered a prayer.

On the charge of the kidnapping of Sarina Basu, do you find the defendant not guilty or guilty?

Guilty. (By now, Miller's grin had faded to a look of complete disbelief.)

With the final verdict rendered Judge Sweeney deferred sentencing until June 29, 1993 and court was adjourned.

As Sheriff's Deputies led Bernard Eric Miller away in handcuffs, his mother, Deborah, bowed her head and fought back tears.

Three of the jurors elected to speak with members of the media and met with them outside of the courthouse in an area designated by Sheriff Michael Chiuchiolo.

The Foreman of the Jury was quoted in the Baltimore Sun as saying; "We considered all the evidence as carefully as we could."

Another juror told Sun reporters that the panel had to take its time considering all the evidence—40 witnesses and more than 160 exhibits.

Jurors also told Baltimore Sun writers that Laurack Bray had a difficult time presenting a defense against a wealth of evidence that was presented in an organized, systematic manner by prosecutors. "The evidence was overwhelming and Mr. Bray's job was very difficult," the foreman said.

Sixteen

Rodney Solomon was anything but a model inmate at the Howard County Detention Center. In the early stages of his confinement he "attempted suicide" by looping a bed sheet around his neck. Corrections Officers removed the sheet and emergency medical personnel responded and rendered first aid. After being interviewed by an institutional psychiatrist he was returned to his cell.

Howard County Detention Center Director, James Rollins, said that Solomon's effort at suicide was simply an attempt on his part to be taken from the security of the center to a location where the possibility of escape would be made easier.

With his unsuccessful suicide try behind him, Solomon decided to cause as many problems as possible at the facility. He began by setting fires in his cell, or using matches and other materials to set off the sprinkler system and flood his cell.

As strange as it may seem, he had a core of followers among Correctional Officers at the detention center. Some were said to idolize him because of his brash, tough guy attitude and actually provided him with contraband items. Following an incident where a fire was started by Solomon, a team of officers took him from his cell, stripped searched him and removed all matches and potential fire hazard materials from his cell. Yet, within a short time span he again had matches and was lighting fires. As no one other than Correctional Officers had access to Solomon, it was certainly reasonable to assume the guards were supplying him with the material.

Solomon and a female inmate "fell in love" after making eye contact in the jail. And that was the only contact possible between the two. They began to exchange love letters with the guards acting as couriers for the two inmates. And indeed this type of action by the guards is strictly forbidden by institutional regulations.

Shortly after their eye contact and "paper love affair" began, the female inmate became a problem. She too set fires in her cell and persisted in other disruptive behavior. A search of her cell turned up the letters from Rodney Solomon, some of which contained instructions on what to do to assist him in creating havoc in the jail.

Solomon would have temper tantrums and threaten anyone who came in contact with him. He assaulted guards by throwing urine and feces on them and he especially enjoyed having them close enough to enable him to throw the substances in their faces. When guards found ways to avoid these almost daily assaults he discovered ways, with inside assistance, to counter. He collected plastic bottles such as shampoo and other hair conditioner containers. He filled them with urine and feces and shook the bottles to create a pasty substance. As officers passed by in the corridor he would use the bottles to shoot the substance into their faces from as far as 15 feet away.

Having had enough of his assaults, Corrections Officers took him from his cell and put him in a straight jacket while they removed the bottles and other contraband. Even then he attempted to assault the officers and was sprayed with pepper mace. He was put into another cell and when he was told that it would be his new home, he threw a tantrum. It was therefore decided to leave him in the straight jacket overnight.

Before supervisory officials who had taken part in the search of his cell could return to their offices, telephone calls from his mother and brother were coming into the jail complaining about the alleged inhumane treatment of Rodney. Once again, this could only mean that one or more of the guards who had taken part in the search had slipped off to notify his family of what had taken place.

Detective First Class Tom Martin made several trips to the detention center to serve papers on Solomon for his assaults on the corrections officers. In Martin's words, "Solomon thought it was a big joke." Although Solomon would refuse to sign the paper acknowledging receipt of them, he would accept his copies.

Solomon filed two separate lawsuits against the Howard County Detention Center and individual officers. He listed among the potential witnesses those correctional officers who were among his hub of worshippers. Much to his dismay, his lawsuits went nowhere.

Rumors of threats on his life continued to filter throughout the detention center and he remained in his isolation cell. One threat, however, came from the outside. An envelope, which obviously contained something, arrived at the jail addressed to Solomon. When the envelope was opened a hangman's noose with a note stating "To Rodney Solomon" was found. There was no evidence whatsoever located that would indicate who might have been responsible for sending the packet.

As his trial date approached, Rodney Solomon was moved from Howard County to the Baltimore County Jail, where he was to stand trial in the Baltimore County Circuit Court.

As prosecuting attorneys made preparations for Solomon's trial, they discussed their list of potential witnesses. In spite of the problems they encountered during Bernard Eric Miller's trial, they agreed to summon Tony Angelo Williams as a State's witness.

On July 1, 1993 the Metropolitan Police Department's Homicide Division notified Sergeant Pete D'Antuono that Tony Angelo Williams was murdered in the District of Columbia on June 25, 1993. His body was then dumped on the Suitland Parkway. Williams' cause of death was listed as multiple gunshot wounds as follows:

        2 bullets to middle of the back
        1 bullet under the chin
        2 bullets to right side of the head
        1 bullet to the back of the head
        1 bullet to the top of the head

The file is still carried by the Metropolitan Police as an open investigation and investigators are continuing to pursue leads in the case. And, of course, there are questions as to whether or not his death was in some way related to his being summoned as a witness against Rodney Solomon.

Seventeen

Rodney Eugene Solomon was tried in Baltimore County before the Honorable Dana M. Levitz and a panel of jurors. Michael Rexrode, Christine Gage and Joseph Murtha appeared on behalf of the State while Samuel Truette, Carol Hanson and Margaret Lanier represented the defense.

With motions hearings behind them, the trial of Rodney Solomon opened with statements from attorneys for the prosecution and defense. The following excerpts are from Mr. Truette's opening statement to the jury.

"Ladies and Gentlemen, Rodney Solomon did not intend for death to befall Pam Basu. He didn't expect it to happen. He did not have control of the events that ultimately resulted in her death.

Bernard Miller drove Pam Basu's car from the point where it was stolen and it was Bernard Miller that operated the car that dragged Pam Basu to her death. Now, Rodney Solomon intended to steal an automobile. That was his intent. That was his purpose—and as soon as he and Bernard Miller went to the I-95 rest area, there is no question about that. And it is not a noble and innocent intent. But that is what his intent was and his intent was not to do injury to anyone.

You will hear that Ms Lagana, who is his first victim, that when Mr. Solomon approached her he went only for her keys. He didn't slap her. He didn't hit her. He didn't wrestle her to the ground. He grabbed her keys. And they tugged and the key chain broke and he had the keys. He went to the driver's side and attempted to start the car. Bernard Miller, however, he grabbed Grace Lagana and thrust her to the ground.

When they went into the Savage area after that and they came into contact and confronted Laura Becraft, once again, Rodney Solomon intending to steal a car went after Ms Becrafts's keys. He had ample opportunity, if he so desired to hit her, to slap her, but when she refused to release those keys, he walked away. And you will also hear that he said to her, "Sorry, Lady." And that will come from Laura Becraft. An interesting aspect of this is that Laura Becraft will say that the most menacing person was Bernard Miller.

Bernard Miller drove the Basu vehicle when he and Rodney Solomon approached that car and removed Pam Basu from that car. If you remember, he drove it because he said he drove it, because when he was arrested by Howard County Police he said, "I drove the car." They went with what he said; "I drove the car. I drove it and I pulled the car over because the child was making too much noise. And I got out and I dropped the child along side of the road. I got back in the car and I continued to drive. And when I reached that sharp curve, I lost it. And I ran into a barbed wire fence and I kept going." That is what Bernard Miller said.

And when they went a short time, short distance after that, at which time Rodney Solomon insisted that he drive because he thought he was going to wreck. He almost did wreck and at that point Rodney Solomon got out of the vehicle, disentangled the body of Pam Basu, and he began driving the automobile. Bernard Miller then became the passenger.

The State Police arrested Rodney Solomon and when they arrested Bernard Miller they took their clothes and they tested their clothes to see what, if any, evidence or blood was on the clothes. Bernard Miller had the blood of Pam Basu on his clothing. Rodney Solomon had no blood of Pam Basu on his clothing.

As far as fingerprints, you all listen to the testimony as far as location of the fingerprints. There are no fingerprints of Rodney Solomon inside the driver's side of the car. The fingerprints are on the outside portion of the vehicle, which is totally inconsistent with what Bernard Miller says.

Now, look, my name is Sam Truette. Carol Hanson, Peggy Lanier and I speak for Rodney Solomon. We are not going to foul the dignity and memory of Pam Basu. We don't seek to intrude upon the grief of Steve Basu and we certainly intend to leave inviolate the love and memories Sarina Basu has for her mother. But we do intend to show you facts that make clear that what the State says occurred just isn't—simply didn't occur. Now, as to the eyewitnesses the State claims they have, I shan't go into the characterization of the eyewitnesses of the abduction of the car and Mrs. Basu, but you all decide for yourselves whether or not they are the type of people you would like to rely upon and who you would base the type of decision which you are all going to be making. You all decide.

And one additional thing; you all are going to hear testimony and you are going to see photographs that are grotesque, that will anger you, alarm you, shock you and inflame you. You are going to hear words coming from witnesses and see photographs that are going to make you want to hate. But look, this little emotion, this visceral effect that these photographs and this case is going to have on you, you all can't enjoy the indulgence of those emotions.

You all are going to have to rise above that. You can't allow the repugnance of what happened, type of death that Pam Basu died, to overwhelm the oath that you took because your visceral reaction, your emotion is not evidence. The photographs are. The testimony is. But your reaction, your horror is not.

Rodney Solomon was there. He did intend to steal Grace Lagana's automobile. He certainly intended to steal Laura Becraft's automobile. And most assuredly, he intended to steal Pam Basu's automobile. But, Ladies and Gentlemen, he did not intend for any death to befall Pam Basu. He certainly didn't intend for any of that to have taken place and it will become totally clear to you that there came a point where Rodney Solomon no longer had control of the events that finally swept up and snuffed out Pam Basu's life."

One of the first witnesses to be called to the stand to testify was Tammy Lynn Rienstra. The following are excerpts from her testimony.

She testified that she left her residence with David Self and Robert Hicks to take her two children to school. On Horsham Drive, they stopped some distance from a car at the Stop Sign and watched a man standing outside of the vehicle. State's Attorney Christine Gage questioned her as follows:

Gage:	What were you watching?
Rienstra:	It appeared to be a man fighting with a woman.
Gage:	What did you see next?
Rienstra:	Fighting, and then somebody running—running to the other side of the car, on the passenger side. And the driver's door opened and there was a woman in the driver's side.
Gage:	Before you go any further... You said fighting. What do you mean by fighting?
Rienstra:	Smacking or punching.
Gage:	Could you describe what happened? What you saw?
Rienstra:	What I saw was one person at the driver's side of the door of the car fighting with the person inside the car. After we saw the

fighting, there was somebody... Another person ran around to the passenger side of the car and got in the door and the door opened and the lady... They pulled... The gentleman at the driver's side pulled the lady out of the car and she landed on her butt.

Gage: You said you know he pulled on her?
Rienstra: He was pulling on her.
Gage: What was he pulling on?
Rienstra: Her shoulders or waist. Something like that.
Gage: Now, when she fell on her butt, what was the man at the driver's side doing?
Rienstra: Getting in the car.
Gage: Before the man at the driver's side got in the car, did you have an opportunity to observe his shoes?
Rienstra: Yes, I did see his shoes. They were white high tops.
Gage: Now, were they all white?
Rienstra: I would say they were all white.
Gage: Could you see the entire shoe or just part of it?
Rienstra: Just part of it.
Gage: How did you know they were high tops?
Rienstra: Because that is what I wear, so I knew they were high tops.
Gage: When the car took off, what happened?
Rienstra: The lady was attached to the car and they drove away with the lady attached to the side of the car.
Gage: Once the car began moving, what did she do?

Rienstra:	She was attached to the car. Her body was bouncing off the ground. Well, first, no. She was running and then there is a dip in the road and that is when her body started bouncing off the road.
Gage:	Where was she running in relation to the driver's window?
Rienstra:	Alongside the car. Alongside of the driver's door.
Gage:	How long did she run?
Rienstra:	Half a second?
Gage:	When she hit the dip in the road, what made contact first with the road?
Rienstra:	Her knees.
Gage:	Do you recall if she had shoes on?
Rienstra:	No, one shoe was off. Her other she was on.
Gage:	After her knees made contact, how long did she stay on her knees?
Rienstra:	She wasn't. She was dragged by her heels and her heels… Only thing I remember seeing, they went straight and we turned and she was being dragged by the heels of her feet.
Gage:	At any time did the car stop?
Rienstra:	No.
Gage:	At this point in time what was your demeanor? How were you feeling?
Rienstra:	I was scared and I was crying. I was just totally… I couldn't believe what I had just seen and I was worried what my kids had seen, because at this time they had done seen everything and they were freaking.
Gage:	Did there come a time that morning when you saw the car again?

Rienstra:	Yes.
Gage:	When did you see the car again?
Rienstra:	Before we got… Before we made the right hand turn into the school.
Gage:	Where were you?
Rienstra:	On Gorman Road.
Gage:	What did you see?
Rienstra:	The same car driving past us down the road and you could see the woman's body still being dragged. She was still tangled or attached to the car and they drove up Gorman Road.
Gage:	And could you see how she was attached to the car?
Rienstra:	What I saw, it looked like her arm was slammed in the door.
Gage:	Did you see any movements of her body?
Rienstra:	No.
Gage:	Did you hear anything as the car moved past you?
Rienstra:	Yes. It sounded like sandpaper or… To me it sounded like sandpaper was being dragged.
Gage:	And in relation to the car, where was the sandpaper sound coming from?
Rienstra:	It sounded like behind it. But you could see the body when you looked. You could see that body being dragged.

Robert Dale Hicks was called and sworn as a witness. Hicks was questioned by State's Attorney Michael Rexrode regarding the events of September 8, 1992.

Rexrode:	What happened that morning?
Hicks:	I came to the… We came to the Stop sign to make our left, I mean our right turn and

	sitting at this Stop sign there was a light colored BMW that two males were beating the woman through the door… Through the window—open window of the vehicle. She was screaming. What happened is we turned the corner and I was in the bed of the truck.
Rexrode:	Let me just ask you one follow up question on that. Where was everyone exactly in the truck?
Hicks:	David, Joey and Tammy were in the cab of the truck. I was riding in the bed of the truck with Michael.
Rexrode:	What kind of truck was it?
Hicks:	Gray Chevy S-10.
Rexrode:	Where was it that you stopped right now?
Hicks:	We stopped at the Stop sign. We had just turned… He stopped about 8 to 10 car lengths back from the BMW.
Rexrode:	He, referring to the driver, David Self?
Hicks:	Yes. He knocked on the window and hollered, Rob. Rob.
Rexrode:	What, if anything, did you do at that point?
Hicks:	At that point I stood up and… I turned around and stood up and looked forward.
Rexrode:	When you looked forward, tell the ladies and gentlemen of the jury what you saw.
Hicks:	Well, when I stood up there was a light colored four door, BMW sitting at the Stop sign. And there were two black males beating the woman through the window—the open window of the BMW and she was screaming the whole time.
Rexrode:	When you say she, who are you referring to?

Hicks:	Pam Basu.
Rexrode:	Where was she in relation to the car?
Hicks:	She was in the driver's seat.

Using a diagram of the car, State's Attorney Rexrode had Mr. Hicks show the members of the jury exactly where Pam Basu was seated in the BMW and where the two other persons referred to in his testimony were standing.

Rexrode:	And what were they doing?
Hicks:	Punching her repeatedly through the open window.
Rexrode:	How were they punching her?
Hicks:	Hard.
Rexrode:	With what?
Hicks:	Their fists.
Rexrode:	How close to the car were they standing?
Hicks:	They were both standing parallel with the vehicle.
Rexrode:	Was the window at the driver's side of the car open or down?
Hicks:	It was open.
Rexrode:	Did you observe anyone else inside the car at the time, except Mrs. Basu?
Hicks:	No, sir.
Rexrode:	How long did these two individuals punch her with their fists?
Hicks:	It was a short time. The whole overtaking of the vehicle only took about 30 seconds. About 30 seconds.
Rexrode:	How hard was she being hit?
Hicks:	Very hard.
Rexrode:	By whom?
Hicks:	By both the black males.
Rexrode:	What happened then?

Hicks:	Okay, at this point, the shorter, lighter skinned black male ran around the front of the vehicle and as the other male opened the driver's door and was pulling her from the driver's seat, the other male opened the other door and was kicking her through the vehicle... Trying to pull her out of the vehicle and he was still... She was still being... He was pulling her and he was kicking her and she was still screaming.
Rexrode:	Let me ask you this, Mr. Hicks. With respect to the individual that was on the driver's side of the car after the other one ran around, what did this individual do after the other one ran around?
Hicks:	Opened the door and was pulling her from the car.
Rexrode:	What did he do once he opened the driver's door?
Hicks:	He grabbed her and yoked her from the vehicle.
Rexrode:	What do you mean by yoking?
Hicks:	Pulled her extremely hard.
Rexrode:	Where did he have her, referring to Pam Basu? How did he have a hold of her?
Hicks:	Grabbed her body, around it... Like around her and he was grabbing her and pulling her.
Rexrode:	Was the back of Pam Basu to his chest as he pulled her?
Hicks:	Pretty much her side he was pulling.
Rexrode:	What happened then?
Hicks:	She came from the vehicle and first she had a grip on the steering wheel. She couldn't hold and she came out of the vehicle.

Rexrode: Let me ask you this. You said she had a grip on the steering wheel. What, if anything, was she doing while this individual was trying to pull her out?

Hicks: Screaming, trying to stay in the car.

Rexrode: How was she trying to stay in the car?

Hicks: By holding on to the steering wheel.

Rexrode: Did you observe that?

Hicks: Yes.

Rexrode: How quickly did she come out of the car and in what manner did she come out of the car?

Hicks: When she finally came out of the car, she flew out of the car and landed on her butt in the street.

Rexrode: She landed in the street. Then what happened?

Hicks: The black male jumped in the driver's seat and closed the door.

Rexrode: Now, the black male that jumped in the driver's seat, which black male was that?

Hicks: Taller, darker skin and heavier man. He was older. Like I said between 27 and 32 years old.

Rexrode: Is that the same person that pulled her out of the car?

Hicks: Yes.

Rexrode: The person who pulled her out of the car and got in the driver's seat, did he ever go to the passenger's side of the car?

Hicks: No, he stayed on that side of the car the whole time.

Rexrode: The individual that went over to the passenger's side of the car, did you ever see that person in the driver's seat?

Hicks:	No, he stayed in the passenger seat the whole time.
Rexrode:	The whole time you observed him?
Hicks:	Whole time.
Rexrode:	Could you describe for the ladies and gentlemen of the jury the person who went to the passenger's side of the car?
Hicks:	Okay. He was young, light skinned. Like about 18 years young.
Rexrode:	Mr. Hicks, I would ask you now to look around the courtroom and I ask you now for the ladies and gentlemen of the jury, if you see in the courtroom either individual… Either individual who got into Pam Basu's vehicle?
Hicks:	Yes.
Rexrode:	Which individual do you see?
Hicks:	That man there.
Rexrode:	For the record, pointing to the individual in the striped shirt and blue tie sitting at counsel for the defense table. The individual you pointed to, Rodney Solomon, did he get into the driver's side of the car or the passenger's side of the car?
Hicks:	Driver's side.
Rexrode:	Once Rodney Solomon got into the driver's side of the car, then what happened?
Hicks:	Pam Basu jumped up from the ground and went back to the car, went back to the driver's window of the vehicle.
Rexrode:	And at this time what was Mr. Solomon in the driver's seat doing?
Hicks:	Punching her out the window. Punching her in the face.

Rexrode:	Where was he at the time he was punching her in the face?
Hicks:	In the driver's seat.
Rexrode:	What happened next?
Hicks:	She was reaching in the vehicle, like she was fighting for some-thing. She was trying to get something. Just reaching in. She jumped right back up and went back to the car.
Rexrode:	She appeared to be reaching for something?
Hicks:	Right. But she was getting hit at the same time.
Rexrode:	By whom?
Hicks:	The driver of the car.
Rexrode:	Then what happened?
Hicks:	She was screaming the whole time and then she grabbed a hold of the vehicle and it started to roll slowly, started to drive off slow.
Rexrode:	Who was driving?
Hicks:	The darker Black male.
Rexrode:	Mr. Solomon?
Hicks:	Yes.
Rexrode:	What happened as it began to leave?
Hicks:	As it began to leave she was holding… She was facing back at us. She was holding with her arm, it looked like in the window—her left arm. And as it started to roll she was still screaming the whole time. She was screaming stop, stop, but it started to go.
Rexrode:	As the car started to drive away, how far was Mrs. Basu from the driver?

Hicks:	A foot away, screaming loud. I could hear her screaming in the back of our truck. Back where we were sitting.
Rexrode:	What was the course of travel of the vehicle?
Hicks:	Straight through the intersection.
Rexrode:	When it was going through the intersection, what could you hear?
Hicks:	Screaming.
Rexrode:	How well could you hear her screaming?
Hicks:	Extremely well.
Rexrode:	Who was screaming?
Hicks:	Pam Basu.
Rexrode:	Where was she in relation to the driver of the car, Rodney Solomon?
Hicks:	She was right in his face. She was stuck to the side... She was holding on at this point only to the driver's door.
Rexrode:	Were you able to continue hearing the screaming?
Hicks:	I heard her scream all the way up until it went back past the park. Until out of sight.
Rexrode:	Okay. Tell the ladies and gentlemen of the jury what happened to Pam Basu as the vehicle got underway.
Hicks:	At first, like I said, she was holding on as the car started to go slow. She was holding on as it started to go slow and there it dips here in the road. There is little dips across the intersection. As it goes across the BMW starts to speed up. As it sped her body fell from the side, but she was stuck to the car. She was screaming when she fell off the car.

	A spray came up from the ground as her body impacted the blacktop.
Rexrode:	Were you able to see this spray?
Hicks:	Yes, sir. It came up and like I said she is… She was flopping like a rag doll stuck to the side of the vehicle and blood just started flying. I still heard her screaming.
Rexrode:	Now, what did the driver of the vehicle, Rodney Solomon, do when she started screaming?
Hicks:	Sped. Sped up. Drove off.
Rexrode:	How fast did the car accelerate?
Hicks:	Very rapidly.
Rexrode:	Once that happened, what happened to Mrs. Basu?
Hicks:	She fell from the side. She was stuck somehow and she was flopping like a rag doll.
Rexrode:	Did you hear anything from what was happening in addition to the screaming? Did you hear her hitting the car or road or anything?
Hicks:	I could hear her scraping. Later I really heard her scraping. At this point I just heard her screaming. I wasn't trying to pick up any other sounds at that time. I was just shocked. When we got to the school I was telling the principal what we saw. I was telling her what was going on and then here comes the BMW right by.
Rexrode:	Describe for the ladies and gentlemen of the jury what, if anything, you observed and/or heard as the BMW traveled along Gorman Road.

Hicks:	I still heard screaming. And I heard as the vehicle was dragging her body—it was making like a skaroo, skaroo noise.
Rexrode:	What kind of noise? If you can mimic the noise, go ahead.
Hicks:	Skaroo. Skaroo. It was just being drug. It was very loud.
Rexrode:	Did you have any difficulty hearing it?
Hicks:	No, I didn't.
Rexrode:	Let me ask you this, Mr. Hicks. How was the car being driven as it went past you?
Hicks:	Fast. It was speeding—like 60 miles an hour. He was going pretty good.

Kevin Brown, the dump truck operator, was called as a witness and told the jury of seeing the assault on Mrs. Basu. During the course of his testimony he identified Rodney Solomon as the man he saw behind the wheel of Pam Basu's BMW.

Trooper First Class Marc Price was called to the stand and told of monitoring a radio transmission by Howard County Police reporting the theft of a vehicle and the murder of its operator during the theft. He told the jury that he later located and pursued the stolen car on Route 108 in Highland, Maryland. His pursuit continued until the vehicle crashed and he apprehended Bernard Eric Miller.

Trooper First Class Steven Proctor testified that he was the assigned Medic on Trooper 8 on the morning of September 8, 1992 and taking part in the search for the stolen BMW. He told jurors of the pursuit of Solomon with the helicopter through a field and his leaving the craft and capturing Solomon. He also told members of the jury that he advised Solomon of his Constitution Rights immediately after his capture.

Officer Jody Tookey was called to testify and told jurors of driving to Gorman road where, "I noticed several people in and around the roadway, screaming and crying and flagging me down. A woman came up screaming as I got half way out of my car."

She spoke briefly with the woman and then began driving in a westerly direction on Gorman Road. "I noticed some kind of mark in the roadway. I didn't know what it was. It was fresh and wasn't there the day before. It was new.

As I continued down Gorman Road, there was a school bus driver standing outside the bus crying and pointing towards Columbia. I said, that way, and she just shook her head in this fashion (nodding) as yes, that way. She couldn't talk. She was hysterical.

As I continued down Gorman Road I passed over I-95 and just beyond 95, over the overpass there appeared to be clothing of some type that looked like it had blood on it. It looked to have been torn and was in the opposite lane from where I was. I then continued down Gorman Road with my lights and siren on. As I came to a very sharp curve I had to slow down. I noticed as I came up to the curve what appeared to be tire marks leading off the roadway into the grassy area. There was fresh damage to a fence and a barbed wire fence post had been knocked down. This fence had not been damaged the day before, September 7th. I momentarily stopped before continuing down Gorman Road. I came up and over a hill, slammed on my brakes and slid over into the other lane."

Rexrode:		Why did you do that?
Tookey:		There was a body in the roadway.
Rexrode:		When you arrived at that particular position, Officer Tookey, exactly what did you observe?
Tookey:		I observed what appeared to be a female lying face down in the eastbound lane of Gorman Road. She was nude from the waist down. The shirt on her back was torn open. Her hands were out to the side and her face

	was down to the side and she appeared to be wrapped in barbed wire.
Rexrode:	What did you do at this point?
Tookey:	I went to check for signs of life. There were none observed.
Rexrode:	What was the condition of her body?
Tookey:	She was mangled. It appeared that her head was gone. You could look inside the skull area and it was an empty cavity.

Mr. Rexrode asked Officer Tookey to view and identify a series of photographs taken on September 8, 1992 of the body of Mrs. Basu. Having established that the pictures fairly and accurately depicted the appearance of the body and the trail leading to it, Mr. Rexrode approached the bench.

Rexrode:	Your Honor, at this time, I am going to place these photographs down for the Court so you can see the other photographs we are not offering. The State would offer State's Exhibit Number 5, the large photograph of Pam Basu.
Lanier:	Naturally, Your Honor, we object.
Levitz:	And you say you are not offering State's Exhibits 129 through 136?
Rexrode:	If I would offer them, I would offer them through the Medical Examiner, if it became probative and relevant through this witness. We are only offering one photograph. However, I wanted the Court to see and be aware of all the photographs we have because we believe that we have eliminated photographs that are the most inflammatory. Certainly they are not the most gruesome of the photographs and I think that's

	particularly true of the next photographs the Court's going to view.
Levitz:	Let me see that one. All right, you want to be heard.
Lanier:	Yes, Your Honor, please. Balancing the probative value against the prejudice it should be excluded. We have no dispute as to the victim's identity, no dispute as to the cause of death. We will stipulate to what her cause of death was. We will stipulate that she died, or the State could prove it through the Medical Examiner, be willing to stipulate that the trail that led up to her body stopped at her body. The photograph doesn't need to be so big, nor does it need to be in color. State has plenty of small photos of her body. The prejudice outweighs the probative value.
Levitz:	Well, I would suggest to you that the small photographs are much worse than the large photograph. The things that are depicted in these small photographs are horrible to look at. They are difficult for anybody to look at. It seems to me that the least prejudicial photograph is the large one that the State intends to introduce. It is benign compared to the things that are shown in some of these other photographs. It accurately reflects the way the victim looked. It's horrible because the crime is horrible. In the sense of what happened to Miss Basu, it accurately reflects how she was found. It is not taken in a way—not photographed in a way to heighten the outrage or the horror that one

would feel if one looked at these photographs, and on balancing it seems to me that the jury is entitled to see the way the victim was found, that it's probative the way the barbed wire is wrapped around her body. It's important to see the condition that she was in when she was found; however, it seems to me that out of all the photographs, it probably is the least inflammatory and the least prejudicial and accordingly I will admit it, State's Exhibit Number 5.

Mr. Rexrode called R. C. Bartley, Forensic Services Supervisor of the Howard County Police Department to the stand to testify. In his capacity as Forensic Services Supervisor Mr. Bartley supervises the Crime Laboratory, the collection and preservation of evidence, the photography lab, the latent fingerprint and inked fingerprint operation, and conducts latent fingerprint examinations in some cases.

Rexrode: Mr. Bartley, could you relate to the ladies and gentlemen of the jury your background, training, knowledge and experience in the area of latent fingerprint comparison and identification as a latent fingerprint expert?

Bartley: As a latent fingerprint examiner I have approximately 21 years experience and prior to that 5 years experience as an inked fingerprint examiner with the Federal Bureau of Investigation. I worked with the FBI for about 16 years before joining the Howard County Police Department. I have testified in 19 different states through-out the United States in Federal, State and Local Courts. I have been qualified in those 19 states as an expert witness. I have approximately 600 hours of classroom training at the FBI Headquarters in Washington as well as their academy in Quantico, Virginia. I routinely teach at the police academy and I have taught at the federal level with the U. S. Attorney's Office and at the state level with the State's Attorney's Office.

At that time Mr. R. C. Bartley was offered and admitted as an expert in the area of latent fingerprint comparison and identification and as a certified fingerprint examiner.

Rexrode: Mr. Bartley, perhaps you could explain to the ladies and gentlemen of the jury the process of fingerprint identification, explaining basically what a latent fingerprint is or a known fingerprint is.

Bartley: The word latent itself implies hidden. Therefore, it takes some type of development to make it readily visible for comparison purposes. Latent fingerprints are associated with crime scene prints. These are developed on nonporous surfaces, glass metal, polished wood, with a variety of fingerprint powders and then lifted with scotch tape lifting tape and put on a card. On paper items we use a number of chemicals that react to different proteins, amino acids present on the paper items or porous items and develop latent fingerprints in that manner. Latent fingerprints are intentionally recorded. This is accomplished by simply applying a thin coat of printers ink on the friction ridge detail on the fingers and rolling the fingers on a contrasting white record type card.

Rexrode: What do you do actually in the process of identifying the finger-prints?

Bartley: Well, you look for characteristics in both the latent fingerprint and the inked fingerprint that line the same unit relationship to the other.

Rexrode: There are a number of people in this room. Do any two of us have the same fingerprints?

Bartley: No, sir. Your fingerprints are formed approximately three months before birth and do not change throughout a person's lifetime, except for natural growth or scarring, either intentional or unintentional scarring.

Rexrode: Do individuals have the same fingerprints on each of their fingers?

Bartley: No, sir. Each finger is unique, including the palms of the hand, the lower joint areas of the fingers and the bottoms of the feet.

Rexrode: Mr. Bartley, I show you what has been admitted as State's Exhibit 146 and ask if you can identify this particular automobile?

Bartley: Yes, I can. This is a car that was placed in the garage under my supervision. It's a BMW covered with mud and we conducted a latent print examination and a couple of other examinations upon.

Rexrode: What did you do to examine this particular automobile?

Bartley: We did a number of things. For one thing, we took a light source and looked for visible prints along the inside of the windows, anything that was visible, so you could apply the powder to that particular area and lift the latent impressions that were obvious. Then we processed the entire inside and outside. We placed a hydraulic jack, which I believe is located back in this area. (Referring to State's Exhibit 146.) At this particular time underneath here, I removed the tire, removed some head hair and some dried blood and bone fragments.

At this time Mr. Bartley explained that he and Crime Scene Technician Doug Read spent days, not hours, processing Mrs. Basu's vehicle. During that time they lifted numerous latent fingerprints from the car.

Rexrode: Did you, in fact, recover any latent fingerprints of Rodney Solomon from that vehicle?

Bartley: Yes, I did.

Rexrode: Where did you recover any prints from?

Bartley: Well, it was from the driver's side, rear passenger door, right below the window.

Mr. Rexrode had Mr. Bartley identify State's Exhibits 102 and 103, which were the latent fingerprint lifted from the driver's side rear door and the inked fingerprint impression of Rodney Eugene Solomon.

Rexrode: What, if anything, did you discover in that impression?

Bartley: That the fingerprint impression appearing in 103, bearing the name Rodney Eugene Solomon and the finger impression, State's Exhibit 102, taken from the driver's side outside surface of the passenger's door, were made by one and the same individual and could not have been made by anyone else.

During cross-examination Mr. Truette asked Mr. Bartley a number of questions concerning the fingerprints on the BMW and the fact that the car had been washed.

Truette: Now, Mr. Bartley, you testified that various surfaces maintain or hold fingerprints better than others, is that right?

Bartley: That's correct.

Truette: Like a smooth surface, nonporous, with a hard finish would be more likely to have latent prints than a porous, rougher surface, is that right?

Bartley: That's what I testified to, sir.

Truette: In addition, you also state that a smooth surface that would contain latent prints, those latent prints would be more easily destroyed.

Bartley: Extremely fragile.

Truette: They would be very fragile?

Bartley: Easily destroyed.

Truette: And you also said that on hard surfaces, like I think you said on the steering wheel of the BMW, you found no fingerprints whatsoever, is that right?

Bartley: That's correct.

Truette: It's grainy, is that correct? Has sort of a grainy, rough surface around the steering wheel?

Bartley: Yes, sir.

Truette: And that doesn't lend itself to maintain fingerprints or latent prints, is that right?

Bartley: Routinely, in the interior of automobiles, we have a lot of trouble developing latent impressions.

Truette:	If a car like this BMW had been taken to a car wash and washed down, first with water, then soap, then a brush run all over it, then rinsed, then waxed with sealer over the wax, then dried, the prints that existed on the surface of the that BMW prior to that type of washing—and you would agree that the BMW surface is a smooth one, is that correct?
Bartley:	Parts of it are, yes, sir.
Truette:	Such a routine would destroy those types of prints, is that right?
Bartley:	It would destroy the majority of just about any print if, in fact, the car wash itself was fully functional and the car had been washed and waxed. If it had been left in a medium of perspiration or oil, if it had been left in perhaps grease, it could possibly endure. Be a small amount of chances of any latent left unless there was maybe one of the brushes didn't touch a particular area.
Truette:	Can you detail prints? Can you tell when a print had been impressed?
Bartley:	You can make an educated guess in the profession. We don't actually say that we can't determine the age of the print. I know that if you washed—if someone were to wash the outside window of their house the night before and then their house was broken into that night and I recovered a lot of fingerprints, I know those prints are one day old. So you can determine, you can make an educated guess in some cases.

Truette:	So that determination is made based upon the fact that you knew there was a clean surface?
Bartley:	Yes, sir.
Truette:	So in this case, this BMW, were you aware of the fact that it had been washed prior to the time that you had processed it?
Bartley:	I was aware of that.
Truette:	Are you aware too, sir, it was washed at a car wash where a brush was used and the brush was used all over the surface of it and soap was used and a rinse was placed upon it and then wax and then a sealant was placed upon it and then it was dried?
Bartley:	No, I was not aware of that.
Truette:	No one described to you the process of the car washing that this BMW went through at that time?
Bartley:	I'm not familiar with the car wash at all.
Truette:	If an adequate job had been done, would you agree it would have removed the fingerprints, the latent prints on the outside of the BMW?
Bartley:	Yes, sir, except, like I said, the medium that it was left and if it was left in anything other than maybe heavy grease or something. I would agree that it would remove fingerprints.
Truette:	It would do a number on any outside prints?
Bartley:	Yes, sir.
Truette:	Fingerprints on the surface of the car in your words are fragile?
Bartley:	Extremely fragile, yes, sir.

Truette:	So based on that, could you then date the fingerprints that you found on the surface of the car?
Bartley:	I couldn't date the fingerprints.
Truette:	Could you say those fingerprints occurred after the washing?
Bartley:	I can't say unless I have seen the individual do the job, okay?
Truette:	In all honesty?
Bartley:	In all honesty.
Truette:	And Mr. Solomon's fingerprints were only found on the right passenger door... Excuse me, left side passenger door of the BMW, is that right?
Bartley:	Driver's side passenger's door, yes, sir.
Truette:	Diver's side, near the driver's door?
Bartley:	Yes, right below the window.

At the conclusion of Mr. Truette's questioning there was a brief redirect examination of the witness by Mr. Rexrode.

Rexrode:	When you powdered that print, did you see any evidence of washing or brush marks around that print?
Bartley:	Well, there appeared to have been a brush mark down the right side through the latent impression itself.
Rexrode:	Would that be the brush mark that could be consistent with washing?
Bartley:	It could be.

When the last witness in the case was called and testimony completed, Judge Levitz gave the instructions to members of the jury. Upon completion of the instructions on Friday, August 13, 1993 prosecution and defense presented their closing arguments to the jury.

Michael Rexrode, speaking on behalf of the State, reminded the jurors of the videotape played for them and the fact that Rodney Solomon on that tape pointed to Pam Basu, as if indicating to Bernard Miller that she is the next victim.

Samuel Truette, in his closing argument as in his opening statement, told the jurors that Rodney Solomon did not intend for Pam Basu to die and that the case was indeed a tragedy.

With closing arguments concluded, the jury left the courtroom to review the facts and evidence presented in the case. It was 5:45 PM when they returned to the courtroom with a verdict.

Levitz:	Madam Clerk, take the verdict.
Clerk:	Yes, sir. Ladies and Gentlemen of the jury, are you agreed upon a verdict?
Jury:	We are.
Clerk:	Who will say for you?
Jury:	Foreman.
Clerk:	Mr. Foreman, please stand. Mr. Foreman, in Case Number 93CR1340, the State of Maryland versus Rodney Solomon, Question 1, Murder in the First Degree of Pam Basu, premeditated; do you find the defendant not guilty or guilty?
Foreman:	Guilty.
Clerk:	Question B, Felony Murder during a robbery, do you find the defendant not guilty or guilty?
Foreman:	Guilty.
Clerk:	Question 3, Robbery of Pam Basu, not guilty or guilty?
Foreman:	Guilty.
Clerk:	Kidnapping of Pam Basu, not guilty or guilty?
Foreman:	Guilty.

Clerk:	Kidnapping of Sarina Basu, not guilty or guilty?
Foreman:	Guilty.
Clerk:	Robbery of Grace Lagana, not guilty or guilty?
Foreman:	Guilty.
Clerk:	Assault with intent to rob Laura Becraft, not guilty or guilty?
Forman:	Guilty.
Clerk:	Thank you. Be seated.

The sentencing of Rodney Eugene Solomon was deferred until August 18, 1993 and court was adjourned.

Eighteen

The savage brutality of Pam Basu's murder, in one way or another, affected people involved with this tragic incident. Some suffered nausea, others experienced insomnia, some lost their appetites and many were haunted by nightmares. What follows are the feelings of these men and women expressed in their own words.

***

"September 8, 1992 was a beautiful day and the beginning of the second week of a new school year. It was the last day of my shift and a day I'll never forget.

I began my shift by picking up a breakfast sandwich and a Diet Coke from Duke's Deli in Elkridge. I drove to the intersection of Route One and Whiskey Bottom Road and parked my car on the lot of the California Inn. I ate my breakfast while listening to the police radio and monitoring the morning rush hour traffic.

Shortly after 8:15 AM I took a call for a reported theft of keys and proceeded to Stephens Road. I arrived at Stephens and Gorman Roads and discovered people everywhere. A woman flagged me down and told me that a car just went up Gorman Road dragging a body. She pointed west and told me to hurry. I radioed the information to the dispatcher and proceeded west on Gorman Road and observed a mark of some type on the roadway surface. As I continued west, and over Interstate 95, I saw a school bus parked on the right shoulder and a woman standing outside the bus crying. I asked her if the car was still going west, but she couldn't speak. She merely nodded her head. As I went on, I noticed bloody clothing lying on the road and I knew then that something terrible had happened. I came to a sharp curve in the roadway and saw what I believed to be tire marks leaving the road and going toward a fence beyond the left shoulder. I could see the fence was freshly damaged and I slowed thinking the victim might be laying in the field. Seeing nothing, I continued along Gorman Road.

I turned a corner and crested a hill in the road. At that moment I had to slam on the brakes and turn to my left. In the middle of the roadway there was a body. The body was nude from the waist down and the shirt was torn up the back. As I went to the body to check for signs of life I saw a car on the side of the road and the driver looking out with a blank stare. I stopped at the body and saw the hole in top of the head and I knew the person was deceased. I radioed the dispatcher and requested immediate assistance.

People were beginning to arrive at the scene and stare at the body. Many of them were screaming at me to do something. I had to make an instant decision to attempt to pursue a car that had already left the scene or remain with the body. I remained with the body and was later told that I'd made the right decision. While people continued to stare at the body I walked to the trunk of my car and took out an emergency blanket. I knew I shouldn't cover the body, but I had to let the woman keep what little dignity she had left.

As I tried to walk over to interview some of the people, I slipped and nearly fell to the ground. It was then that I realized that the mark in the roadway was from her body and that I had just slipped in her blood. I was later relieved of my duties at the crime scene and expected to return to my regular assignment as if nothing had happened.

Two days after the murder I sat down to dinner and suddenly became sick. I couldn't touch my food because I could only see her body lying there in the road. And sometimes my stomach still turns.

I had nightmares for days. I saw the victim standing in the roadway asking me for help. She would yell at me to do something and her child would cry. In the days before the first trial, I had the nightmares again. I still have the horrible dreams, but not as often. People tell me I'll always have them.

I've never had any contact with Pam Basu's family and, in some ways, I'm not sure that I'd ever want to. Someday I might feel differently. But I often pray that somehow her family will put their lives back together.

For me, not a day goes by that I don't, in some way or another, think of that homicide on a Tuesday morning in September."

Jody A. Tookey
Police Officer
Howard County Police Department
***

"My First thought as I was dispatched to a residence off of Horsham Drive to check on a child that was thrown from a vehicle was, 'Why me?' I hadn't heard of any serious accident and the address was well out of my assigned area in Columbia. In addition, I was perplexed that Police Dispatch advised that the Fire and Rescue Services were not on the way for a child tossed from a car. My confusion only increased when I switched my radio to the other channel, as my ears were met with frantic and jumbled radio transmission. Little did I know that I was on my way to a horribly brutal crime that would gain national attention.

I went first to a residence to check on the little girl and then to Horsham Drive and Gorman Road. There I observed a darkened red streak on the pavement heading in a westerly direction and clumps of hair. I knew that I was looking at part of a crime scene, but didn't know how big it was at this point. I just knew that it was very serious. As I listened to the radio transmissions, I began to get a sharper picture of what had occurred. I learned that a woman named Basu had her vehicle stolen and she was somehow dragged to her death, and her child was tossed from the vehicle. However, as far as I was concerned, I was just there to secure a part of the crime scene. The last thing I expected that morning was for a man who said he was Mr. Basu to pull his vehicle up beside me and say, 'Excuse me, Officer. I'm looking for my wife who was supposed to be following me. Can you help?' I'll always remember those words.

A thousand thoughts raced through my mind in a split second. I had never made a death notification before and was in no way prepared to make one then. I knew too little about the facts and was very afraid of giving Mr. Basu misinformation. At that point I wanted and needed guidance. In an effort to gain a short moment for my thoughts, I told Mr. Basu to turn his vehicle around and park behind me. As I instructed him, the look on his face told me that he knew exactly what I was going to tell him. As he was turning his vehicle around I radioed and asked a supervisor to respond and help me. None answered my call.

For reasons I don't know, I can't remember my exact words to Mr. Basu. I do know that I was very sad for him and I felt extremely helpless. He wanted to know details that I simply didn't have, and this left him with so many unanswered questions.

After he composed himself I escorted Mr. Basu to see his daughter. There we were met by someone who offered instant relief, a Fire Department Chaplain. He took over consoling Mr. Basu and I returned to my post.

To this day I think about the Basu murder every time I drive down Gorman Road. I still recall the feeling of loneliness as

I made the death notification and hope that others will never have to experience it.

To the credit of the Commanders of the Howard County Police Department all of us involved in that horrible incident that day is a survivor. They arranged for, and insisted that everyone involved in the case attend a group session with Doctor Jeff Mitchell at the end of the day. It allowed me to air my frustrations and state how I felt about the entire incident.

I often think about that day and the events that took place, and I continue to feel sorrow for the Basu family and hope that no one ever again will have to experience such a tragic death."

Brook Donovan
Police Officer
Howard County Police Department

***

"Since that day in September, whenever I look at a BMW or hear the word carjacking, whether I read about it occurring in California or locally, I think of the sad unforgiving way Mrs. Pam Basu died. The graphic pictures of Mrs. Basu with barbed wire wrapped around her lifeless body are permanently etched in my mind. I worked for seven years at a Maryland State Police Barrack along the I-95 corridor and have been exposed to many fatal accidents. None of those past fatal accidents can compare to the lifeless body I saw in those photographs. Many of my friends and co-workers asked the same question, 'Did you see her body at the scene?' My response has always been, 'No, thank God. The photographs were bad enough.'

I have a daughter who at the time of the carjacking was one and a half years old, close in age to that of Mrs. Basu's daughter. After arriving home, I picked up my daughter and hugged her and my wife. It seemed to be one of the longest hugs I've ever given.

I can remember while driving home that evening I said a prayer for Mrs. Basu. My thoughts at the time were how sorry I felt for Mrs. Basu and I prayed that nothing like that would ever happen to my wife and daughter.

It's puzzling how two human beings can commit such a horrendous crime and think to themselves that they could get away with it. It angers me to know a person could toss an innocent child out of a vehicle like she's some piece of litter.

I can still see the faces of the accused during my segment of testimony, sitting in the chair next to counsel with no sign of remorse or guilt. No remorse at all over how they took the life of Mrs. Basu. And I ask, where is the justice? They didn't receive the death penalty, only life in prison. The attorneys for the State, Mr. Rexrode, Mr. Murtha and Mrs. Gage proved their guilt beyond a reasonable doubt. Where is the justice?"

Marc W. Price
Trooper First Class
Maryland State Police
***

"The events of September 8, 1992 are forever etched in my mind. Rarely does a day go by that I don't think about the senseless murder of Pam Basu. Ironically, my new assignment as a Patrol Sergeant has me working the same area where the murder occurred. Several times a shift I drive by the memorial to Pam on Gorman Road that was arranged by her family and friends.

I am very proud of the teamwork that went into the apprehension, interrogation and the successful prosecution of Solomon and Miller. I cannot say enough about the fine work done my by colleagues with the Howard County Police Department, the men and women of the Maryland State Police, The FBI, the prosecution team of the Howard County State's Attorney's Office and, most of all, the citizens of Howard County who came forward and provided vital information on the murder of Pam Basu. I must say, however, I was extremely disappointed that Solomon was not sentenced to death. I feel the criminal justice system let the Basu family and the citizens of Maryland down."

Thomas Martin
Sergeant
Howard County Police Department
***

"The primary purpose of the helicopter is medical evacuations. Although we will get involved in other types of search and rescue operations, our job mainly is Medevac.

On September 8, 1992 we received a call to assist Howard County in a search for a BMW stolen during a carjacking. Initially, we had very little information about the case. We knew a car had been stolen and there was a death involved and that one of the suspects was possibly armed with a handgun.

As we flew over the area to begin our search I remember looking down and seeing the body lying in the roadway. That was as close as we got to the body. Of course, I've been flying Medevac missions for almost 20 years and the blood and death have become part of my everyday life.

While conducting the search for the stolen car, we heard TFC Price say he had the vehicle in sight. Once in the area we could see a suspect fleeing across an open field toward a heavily wooded location. No ground units were even close to the individual and if he had gotten into the woods he might have escaped capture. Scott set the helicopter down and I jumped out and began chasing the suspect. At the time I was thinking about the information that the suspect may have a handgun. I knew a death was already involved in the incident and I was out in the open and not wearing body armor. We don't normally wear body armor while flying. I drew my weapon and ordered the suspect to halt, but he continued to run. I made up my mind that if he turned suddenly toward me I was going to shoot him. Finally, he went to the ground, but wouldn't follow orders. He placed his arms under his body and refused to take them out and place them to his sides as ordered. I was able to pull his arms from under him and place the handcuffs on him just as other units began to arrive.

It wasn't until he was in custody that I learned the full details surrounding the incident. After hearing of how the woman died and the little girl being thrown from the car, I thought I could have shot him and still slept good that night.

It's very rare, because of my assignment that I get a chance to arrest and cuff a suspect. It felt especially good to make this apprehension and I had a deep sense of personal satisfaction."

Steven Proctor
Maryland State Police

***

"Usually our function is to provide a support role to ground units. We provide them with information as to location of suspects and they make the apprehensions. In this case, however, there were no ground units in position to make the arrest.

In most cases the suspect will fall to the ground and surrender when we put the helicopter over them. I maneuvered in front of this suspect and turned the helicopter so we were facing him, but he wouldn't stop. He just kept running. I saw an opportunity to land and I took it. Steve jumped out and began pursuing the suspect and I took off again. I thought it better to stay in the air just in case Steve didn't apprehend the guy. I could keep him in sight until ground units converged on the area to make the arrest.

Of course, we have to be very careful when there's a chance that the suspect is armed. We are just a big target in the sky for them. We can't take unnecessary chances and risk being hit by gunfire.

One irony in this case is that if Steve had shot the guy, he would've then had to treat him. After treating him, we'd have to load him on the helicopter and fly him out for medical treatment. This is probably the closest we've ever been to doing that.

If we hadn't been there, the suspect probably would've escaped, because no ground units were close enough to capture him. In this case, it felt good to say that be being there we made a difference."

Scott Richardson
Maryland State Police
***

"It's been more then a year since the trials of Bernard Eric Miller and Rodney Solomon and, even now, one is still haunted visualizing the videotape of a mother and daughter waving a final goodbye to a proud and unsuspecting father. And Bernard Miller and Rodney Solomon are viewed lurking in the background. Only a few minutes later the same Bernard Miller and Rodney Solomon would savagely beat Pam Basu, kidnap Sarina and unmercifully and wantonly drag Mrs. Basu to her death only a short distance from her home. This brutal act would shock the sensibilities of our county, our state and even our nation.

And yet, after two long trials, troubling questions still remain. What causes a Bernard Miller and Rodney Solomon to suddenly undertake an extended crime spree in lieu of calling for help from the rest stop location when their car ran out of gas? Why would they seize a car knowing an infant child was in the backseat? And, most of all, why didn't the driver, Rodney Solomon, simply stop the car instead of dragging Pam Basu to her death? Only Rodney Solomon and Bernard Miller can answer these and other questions. What we can only say is, that the tragic death of Pam Basu has raised our collective consciousness to the horror of violent crimes occurring even near our homes.

Undoubtedly, Doctor Pam Basu's violent death resulted in both state and federal carjacking legislation. And, ultimately, every would-be carjacker should now know that the 16-year-old passenger/accomplice, Bernard Miller, is serving a life plus sentence in a Maryland Penitentiary. The driver, Rodney Solomon, will serve the remainder of his natural life in prison without the possibility of parole."

Michael Rexrode

Howard County State's Attorney's Office
***

"On September 8, 1992 I was called to Howard County Police Headquarters to be briefed on what appeared to be a very bizarre and gruesome murder. As I traveled to the police department, I was unaware of the fact that I was soon to become part of something that would not only have an incredible impact upon my life for the coming year, but also be party to an event that would stay with me for years, possibly even my life. That event was the tragic and gruesome death that was suffered by Pam Basu and my role in seeing that the two men responsible for her death were punished for their crime.

From the moment of Pam's death, to the evening almost a year later when Rodney Solomon was sentenced to life without parole, not a day went by that I wasn't in some manner involved in the ongoing preparation for the trial of Bernard Miller or Rodney Solomon.

I find it hard to encapsulate in a brief statement all the days, evenings, nights and weekends that were spent on trial preparation. There were endless witness interviews, legal research, trial exhibits to be put together, legal motions to be filed and argued, and continuing 'what ifs' in an effort to be prepared for any possible situation when we eventually went to trial. I clearly recall the undying devotion of my colleagues, Mike Rexrode and Christine Gage. Our lives were dedicated to the pursuit of making sure that Pam Basu's killers were not only convicted, but also severely punished.

Under the learned guidance of Mike Rexrode, we charted a course of strategy and embarked on one of the most notorious prosecutions in the history of Howard County. Scrutinized by the watchful eye of media from around the country, we worked incredible hours and spared no expense to make sure that when we walked into court in April and August 1993, we knew we had done everything humanly possible to ensure that justice would be served.

These two cases represented a year's devotion of my life. As a prosecutor, I am incredibly proud of my contribution to the trials of both Bernard Miller and Rodney Solomon. As a human being, removed from the professional image that was necessary to the prosecution of the cases, I still feel the terrible sadness that was always present during the trial. Yes, there was anger and outrage, but more than anything there was sadness. The sadness of Steve Basu, Pam's husband. The sadness of meeting little Sarina and knowing that she represented much of what Pam lived for and everything that she died for. I felt the sadness with every friend and relative that I met. Whether it was Pam's sister, Nita, her father, mother, friend or relative, no matter whom it was, the presence of looming sadness was cast about the room. Often on the verge of tears, I embraced the sadness to fuel the passion, which motivated me throughout the two trials. But more than anything else I felt the sadness of never having the opportunity to meet the woman who captured the hearts of every person she met.

The incredible professional challenge that being involved in the prosecution of a notorious case presented seems to be the most indelible image that I recall when reflecting upon the trial. Despite the long hours and the endless tasks associated with the trial, I believe I matured as a trial lawyer and a prosecutor. Much of that growth was as a result of having had the guidance of such a brilliant prosecutor as Mike Rexrode to lead the trial team of Christine Gage and myself. It is because of Mike's leadership and skill that we successfully prosecuted Bernard Miller and Rodney Solomon. I am proud to have had the opportunity and the honor to be co-counsel with Mike Rexrode.

Finally, I would be remiss not to mention the incredible compassion and support that I felt from Pam's family and friends. Despite their sadness and daily struggle to deal with the tragic loss of Pam, I always felt the warmth of their personalities. I believe that my life has been touched forever as a result of meeting Pam's family. And despite the fact that Pam's life was cut short by such a tragic and gruesome event, I know that her spirit lives forever in the hearts and souls of the people she touched. I feel honored to have had a chance to be touched by people who Pam loved so dearly. I pray that they may find peace and serenity in their lives."

Joseph Murtha
Howard County State's Attorney's Office

Nineteen

With the trials finally over and days of anguish and mind searing anticipation behind them, a family still grieves the loss of a daughter, a sister, a wife and mother. Only their words can tell us of their pain and suffering and even then, there can be no words to truly express the emptiness, the loneliness of such a tragic loss.

***

"Our youngest daughter, Pam, a loving, caring, self-confident, self-sacrificing and above all a fun loving person was dragged to her death on September 8, 1992. The news of this tragedy, when conveyed to us in India, shattered our lives forever and those of our remaining three daughters. Throughout our long journey to the United States, we were painfully reminded of the tragedy, as the news was covered around the globe. Upon our arrival we were not fortunate enough to pay last homage to our child's mutilated body for obvious reasons.

God has created parents with a mind and soul, filled with nurturing feelings and ones that cannot see their children suffering even from minor injuries. In an effort to feel the excruciating, gruesome pain and agony that were thrust upon our child, we trekked the two miles on Gorman Road and reached the spot where our child's body was dislodged from the car. Mentally and physically, wrecked we returned in a state of confusion wondering, 'why us?'

Generally, after the funeral the healing process starts they say. For us it was the start of our intense and intolerable pain and anger towards the individuals who were truly responsible for her dreadful killing. We did not know the facts revealed during the trial of Bernard Eric Miller earlier. The Medical Examiner's report and the photographs and sketches presented during the trial added fuel to the smoldering fire and brought severe mental agony to us, followed by nightmares that there are no words to express. What has been taken away from us is the most anyone can take from another person—our lives. We ask is there any punishment equal to what these individuals did to our child? Intense and compelling protective urges for our child make us feel guilty for our absence on the scene when our child was mercilessly dragged to her death.

Prior to this incident, we were always God fearing and had staunch faith in His mercy. These beliefs and life long experience had given us strength as we both approached our retirement life. After this incident, our faithless minds have started questioning God's judgment in bringing such a tragic and horrible death to our innocent child. We know and admit that God is not answerable to humans for His actions. This leaves us with a feeling of deep helplessness and resorting to fate—destiny.

Our frequent visits to Pam's house to see Sarina and Steve bring back the dreadful memories of our daughter traveling those roads and environment that brought her merciless death. An hour-long drive to her house brings us intense pain, which is to some extent compensated by the smiles and playfulness exhibited by Sarina. Prior to this incident these same roads and environment were a source of pleasure and peace for us when we visited Pam and her family.

Watching Sarina grow up gives us the greatest pleasure, but not without a sense of hurt at the same time, that Pam was not blessed to enjoy the days so precious to parents. As when we go shopping, we watch the crowd with a hope to find our Pam somewhere out there. We return with our hopes and dreams shattered and forever questioning, Merciful God, Our Lord, why did you forsake our child? We attend compassionate friends meetings, join aggrieved parents and light candles with no relief whatsoever to our mind and souls.

We were the proud parents of four lovely daughters, two of whom live in India with their families. Pam and our daughter, Nita, here in the U. S., always planned our retirement such that we could be close to the youngest grandchildren—Sarina and Sean. It will not be the same without her. Pam was an inspiration to us and always made us feel young and strong. Her death has left us feeling defeated, physically exhausted and guilty that we do not have it in us to provide the support, love and care needed by our remaining daughters and all our grandchildren."

Pam's sister, Nita, said, "How can I begin to articulate the loss? A life so abruptly and viciously ended, a life that had so much more to give—a life so precious to me. Pam wasn't just a sister; she was my friend, someone with whom I had shared a lot and there was a lot more to come. We went to boarding school together in India. We came to this country together. She was to be my only family in this country and she was to take care of our son should something happen to my husband and I. Her selfless devotion to make the world a better place, her passions for science and children are all lost when there were so many contributions she was to make. Her loss is going to be felt not only by her family, but also by relatives, friends, colleagues near and far whose lives she touched in her own very special way.

I ache when I wake in the middle of the night, as I have done many times over the past several months. There is this sinking feeling as I long to hold my sister, to hug her, to tell her, I love you, Pammy, to see her beautiful smile, to watch those big black eyes sparkle back at me and mostly to hear her giggle. Then I realize I will never again have the pleasure I had grown accustomed to in the last 34 years. Pam will never again be alive. I lay awake the rest of the night thinking of the impact of the senseless tragedy that took Pam away from all of us. I feel saddened, angry, discouraged and very helpless. I have come to the painful realization that our lives have forever been diminished, the lives of Sarina, Bishu, my parents, my sisters, my husband, my son and me.

I am sad even when I am happy and joyful as I listen to Sarina's laughter and watch her acting out all the nursery rhymes she can now recite. On September 8th when I picked her up she was talking in two words sentences. 'Man boo boo. Mamma fall.' Today Sarina pieces the sequence of events on that horrible morning as follows: 'Bad man hit Mamma. She not hold my hand. She fall down. Mamma gone to heaven. I not go to heaven. I stay here with daddy.' We hope that she will overcome the trauma and grow and develop into a happy, bubbly, spirited little person. It saddens us to know that Pam will never have her dreams of motherhood fulfilled, or of watching all of Sarina's upcoming accomplishments. I ache when I realize that Sarina has forever been denied those special hugs from her Mamma to her Precious for every little accomplishment and disappointment. Many times I walk over to my answering machine in anticipation of a message from Pam. 'Hi, Nita, your little Pookie just painted the entire kitchen floor with her little finger-paints. Thought you would like to know.' I am not only disappointed when reality hits, but I ache because I will never again hear the excitement and passion in her voice.

I watched my brother-in-law testify at the trial. I felt the pain he felt as he went through the event, something we both have talked about many times. I am tormented when he says, 'How can this be? After 12 years our lives were just coming together. We have a family and now it's all gone.' Instead of being happy when he lands a new business contract, he is deeply saddened. 'It's getting closer to fulfilling Pam's dreams, but she is no more,' he says. He shakes his head in utter defeat. I don't want to think of the pain she must have felt, how afraid she must have been. We hug and cry and hold each other to comfort ourselves, both in our own way wishing we could tell Pam that her little Precious and Pookie, Sarina, is okay.

I ache when my parents sob their hearts out, all the time shaking their heads and asking, 'Why?' At 74 my father has given up all hope and beliefs. No parent should ever have to experience the death of their child. My parents lost their youngest of four, the one on whom they relied for all emotional support. I am bitter when I see my mother totally devoid of energy, doing her utmost to care for Sarina when she visits them. 'She is all we have left of Pam,' she says and carries on. Their lives have been changed drastically at a time when they were settling down to retirement. I have no words or actions to comfort them.

I am outraged that two human beings could put their desire for a hunk of metal on par with my sister's life. The mindlessness of their actions, their refusal to stop when the situation had gone too far, their risking of Pam's life and then taking it with total disregard, is so incomprehensible that all things that are sacred, sure, that give my life purpose are now adrift, distrusted and unsure. There is a pall on every minute of every day. A future that was rich in expectations for my sister and I—for our family—is numb, empty, lost. And while time will heal some of this, and day-to-day distractions will bring my life back to the norm, I will reach for the phone every now and then as I did the other day, and know that my life is diminished. My sister is gone and I am less forever."

Pam's husband, Steve, would say, "How completely the killing of my wife and near killing of our daughter, Sarina, has shattered my life and Sarina's life. Every time I think of it, a total numbness comes over me. My chest starts to hurt, my heart begins to sink, my eyes become full of tears and my hands start shaking.

A sense of loss, grief, void and helplessness overwhelms me and robs me of all my energy.

I often wonder if God had fallen asleep allowing this to happen, or was it God's wish to take a loving, gentle soul away from this world, a mother from a child, a wife from her husband, a sister, a daughter and a friend so violently, so painfully. I do not know.

Everyday when I drive the asphalt road, I see Pam's broken limbs, her blood soaked clothes. I hear her crying in fear and pain. Arriving at the Stop sign only 50 feet from my doorstep I can almost feel the chill Pam must have felt as the two men approached her, feel the blows as they beat her, hear her cries as she struggled to rescue Sarina while the car speeds up, dragging her along side. I hear the thud of her head hitting the pavement and I can almost hear the life going out of her.

Imagine reliving this everyday and having your two-year-old daughter describe this to you in vivid detail every time you pass that intersection. Each day, when the night falls from the sky, I hold my daughter and tell her and myself that this is only a nightmare. Tomorrow we will wake up in the sunshine, walk to the silver creek, stand under the tree holding hands, and her Mamma will come to us from the sky and meet us. She will smile at us, hold our hands and we will all be together. But tomorrow never comes.

My daughter wakes up in the middle of the night crying for her Mamma and walks through the house looking for her Mamma. I pick her up and as we stand in a pool of tears at our feet, we look at her picture and try to listen for her voice in the gentle wind outside.

Our house was made a home by my wife. Pam struggled for many years to have a child. Then she fought every obstacle to adopt our daughter from a distant land and bring her home. Now I have only questions. I ask why should anyone give life to a child only to die so senselessly. Pam never hurt anyone.

Since Pam's killing, I am haunted by the images of my daughter surrounded by a pair of vicious men and my wife dying in the gutter. I will never be released from these walls of horror, grief, sorrow, loneliness and pain. The path of my daughter's life will never be brightened by her Mamma's beaming smile. My daughter, Sarina, has been given the ultimate sentence of life without her Mamma. My wife's cries are on this rock hard, dirty asphalt, in the green grass, the trees and in the gentle wind."

Twenty

On June 29, 1993 Bernard Eric Miller was given a life sentence for his part in the killing of Pam Basu. The sentence allows for parole in 18 years. On August 18, 1993 Rodney Eugene Solomon was sentenced to life in prison without the possibility of parole.

Sadly, the only death sentence in this case was handed down and carried out on September 8, 1992 by Rodney Solomon and Bernard Miller when they murdered Pam Basu.

No words can be found in any dictionary, within the civilized world, that can describe the brutality of Pam Basu's death. The snuffing out of an innocent life by any means is in and of itself brutal. But to be dragged to death, trapped by the seatbelt of her own car, while trying to rescue the child she so dearly loved, is unimaginable.

***

"Much has been written about the heinous nature of this crime spree, so I will forego elaborating on that aspect.

Crimes of this nature touch home to all involved, because it instills concerns for all members of society who are not street conscious, or who believe this couldn't happen to them. It expresses our vulnerability and the end result is being wary. 'Is your car door locked?' Something I ask my wife each and every time she's driving.

Bernard Miller and Rodney Solomon didn't receive the death penalty in the State of Maryland. However, I sincerely hope they realize they still have one more Judge, the Supreme Judge of mankind, to face for their actions on a day in September."

R. C. Bartley
Forensic Services Supervisor
Howard County Police Department

Twenty-One (Photo Galley)

Doctor Pam Basu, who was dragged to death while attempting to rescue her 22-month old daughter, Sarina, is shown here at her desk at Alcoa.

Pam and Steve on their wedding day July 7, 1980

Pan and Steve, vacationing in 1982

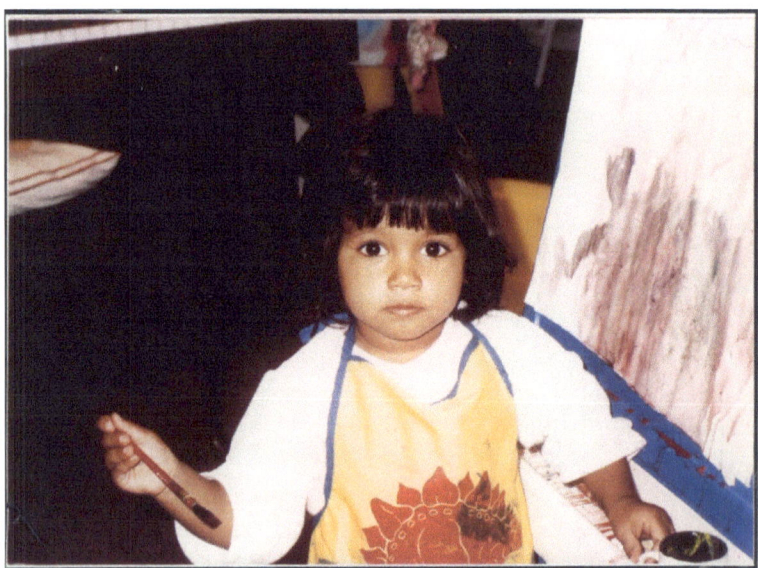

Twenty-two month old Sarina was thrown from the car and left on the side of Gorman Road.

Sarina at six-years of age.

Sarina, age 16.

Pam with her father, 1988.

The 1976 Cadillac out of gas on Interstate 95, driven by Rodney Eugene Solomon and occupied by Bernard Eric Miller.

Bernard Eric Miller's blood-stained tee shirt lying on the side of Gorman Road.

Bernard Miller at the time of his arrest on 09-08-92.

Rodney Eugene Solomon immediately after his arrest.

Arrow indicates body drag marks on Gorman Road.

Arrow indicates damaged road marker, which was struck when the victim's car was driven off the roadway.

Arrow indicates body drag marks reentering the roadway after the suspects intentionally struck the fence in an effort to dislodge the victim's body.

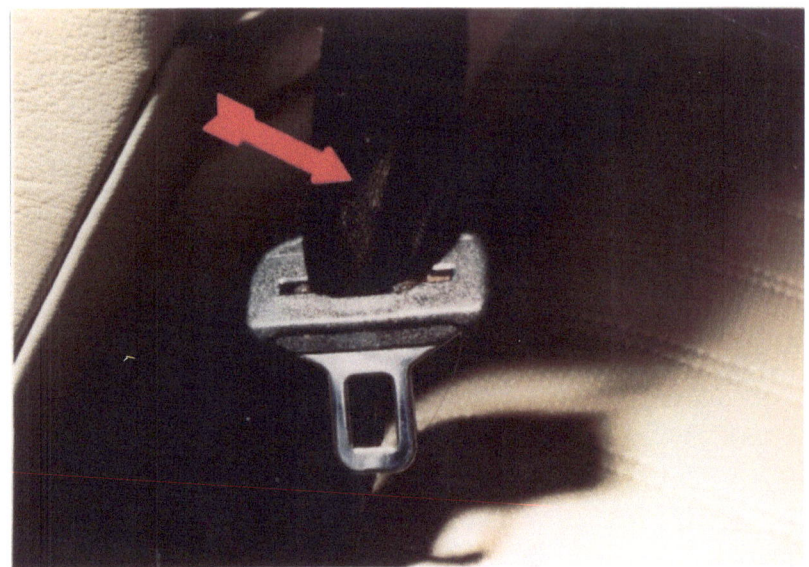

Skin and tissue of the victim on the seatbelt

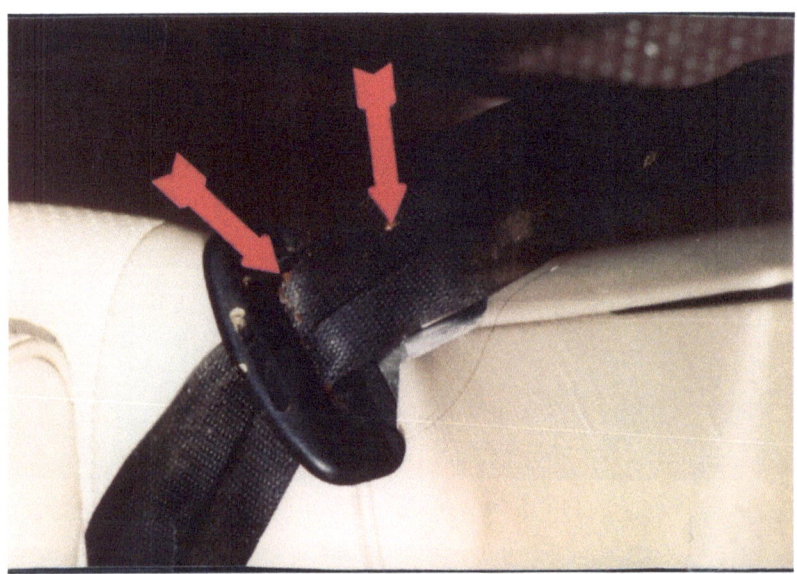

Blood and tissue fragments on the seatbelt.

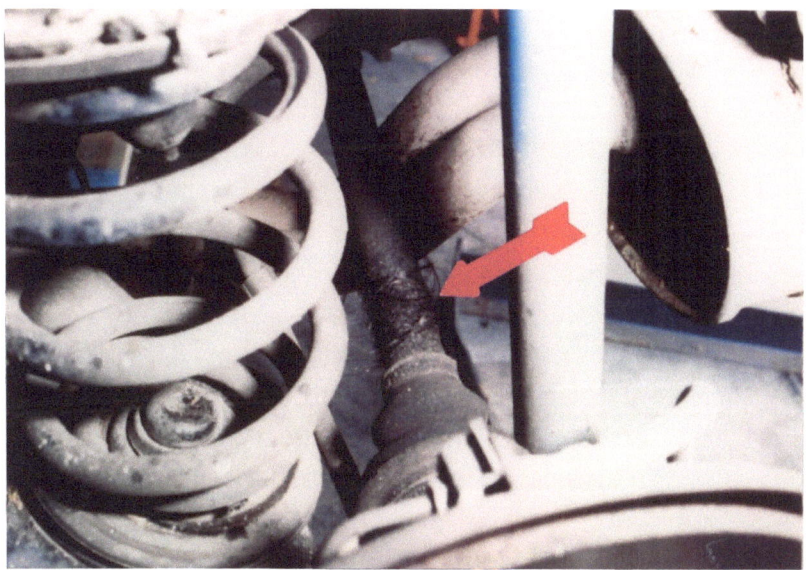
Victim's hair, which had been pulled through the left rear wheel and entwined around the axle.

Scott Richardson (left) was the Pilot of Trooper 8 on September 8,1992 and Steven Proctor (right) was the medic who exited the helicopter and apprehended Rodney Solomon.

Epilogue

There was a sudden and drastic change in our lives—Sarina's and mine, after Pam's death. You don't expect things like this to happen and there was an almost crushing emptiness, a loneliness that is very difficult to describe. Pam was always there for Sarina and I, and I didn't know my life without her. So many adjustments had to be made, but we had a lot of help. Pam's sister became almost a surrogate mother.

I recall the sleepless nights and the terrible nightmares that Sarina had over and over again. Even though she was so young at the time, she remembered everything that happened that morning. So many nights I slept on the floor beside her bed to be there for her when she had the dreams.

Seeing what happened to her mother haunted her even during her waking hours. She developed a dreadful fear of African American men, and this caused me a great deal of anguish because I had a very dear and trusted friend, Russell, who was African American. I took her to have her picture taken, and the photographer was a young African American man, and she was terrified. It took time to work through her fears and learn that there was good and bad in every race. Friends and family—Pam's mother and sister, were there to help her through those times. The good people who surrounded Sarina not only helped her, but also helped me. That's how we survived the first few years.

There was a time too, when I was with Sarina in the mall. A woman approached me and said what a beautiful little girl Sarina was. She said she could get Sarina into commercials and gave me a business card and asked for my telephone number. A few days later she called and asked again about having Sarina in commercials. She seemed most anxious about this, and it was during the conversation that I realized that she now knew who

Sarina was and what she had been through. I suddenly felt that my daughter would be exploited because of someone's greed and I declined the offer. I couldn't do that to Sarina or to Pam's family.

As time passed, Sarina surprised me with her insight into my feelings. She would help around the house, but I never asked her. She even began doing the laundry on her own and seemed very content doing it. I think she did it to help me.

She did surprisingly well in school, but I'm certain she got her tenacity and dedication from Pam. She got very good grades and became a member of the National Honor Society and a Merit Scholar. After graduating from Mt. Hebron High School she was accepted at Georgia Tech. At first, she wanted to study architecture, but after attending the pre-class seminars she decided to change her major to engineering. She wanted to become an Industrial Engineer, but was told she would have to take classes in General Engineering for the first year to determine if she had the knowledge and ability to transfer to Industrial Engineering. Thirty-five percent of the students would drop out by the end of the first semester, and by the end of the second semester, sixty-five percent of the original enrollment would drop out. Sarina prevailed with a 3.6 GPA and is now enrolled in the Industrial Engineering classes.

As for me, I still haven't found complete closure. I haven't been able to put Pam's death behind me. I think it will always be there to haunt me in some way. It has to be the way she died—so sudden and so brutal. I went to counseling for a while, hoping it would help. But I stopped going. I don't know why. I've thought about going back again, but so far I haven't been able to do it. Maybe one day I will.

It seems strange—and I still remember this, but I met Pam on September 9, 1977. I met her on September 9th and I lost her on September the 8th, fifteen years later.

Pam was so happy on the morning of September 8th. Sarina's very first day of pre-school and Pam was on Cloud 9. She wanted me to videotape everything, and I knew we would be showing the film to family and friends over and over. She was smiling and so proud of our little girl when she walked out to the car to take her to school. I can still see her smiling as she put Sarina in the car. Then—and then she was gone.

            Steve Basu

Appendix A

Appendix A is included to show the discrepancies and a number of constants in the statements of Bernard Eric Miller. It gives readers the opportunity to compare their thoughts and notes with those of the investigators who worked the case.

Miller Statements

Statement #1:	Comment at arrest scene	09-08-92
Statement #2:	Oral statement at HCPD	09-08-92
Statement #3:	Taped statement at HCPD	09-08-92
Statement #4:	Oral statement at HCDC	09-09-92
Statement #5:	Taped statement at HCDC	09-09-92
Statement #6:	Oral statement at HCPD	09-10-92
Statement #7:	Taped statement at HCPD	09-10-92

Statements one through seven will be referenced in this addendum, although statements one, three, five and seven were quoted exclusively in the text. The purpose for the including all of the statements is to show the varying accounts given on each occasion by Miller.

TOPIC: Who was driving the BMW was it was initially stolen from Pam Basu?

Statement #1 (Oral):
1. Rodney took her car.

Statement #2 (Oral):
1. Rodney then pulled around the corner and said, 'Get in. Get in.'
2. When Rodney pulled up to him, Rodney was rushing him to get in the car saying, "Get in. Get in."
3. Rodney pulled off real fast and hit something.
4. Rodney stopped the car because the baby was crying.

Statement #3 (Taped):

1. I was waitin' for him. Next thing I know he pulled around and said, 'Get in.'
2. I was drivin' the car.
3. Me and Rodney, we was drivin'. He was sittin' on, I think he was sittin'. The lady was hooked up.
4. Yeah, I started the car.
5. And then that's when he just said move over and he just started drivin'.
6. But I ain't never press on the gas though.
7. I just started the car. Just sit there.
8. Then he pushed me over and pulled off with the lady still... She was still hung up in there.
9. No, he said um, he say, who crashed the car? But we crashed the car when Rodney was tryin' to get me out the seat.
10. Question: And when you hit the fence, who was driving?
   Answer: Me.
11. Question: Okay, and where was Rodney?
   Answer: On top of me. Pushin' me out the way.
12. I wasn't holdin', I wasn't holdin' the steering wheel.
13. Yeah he was... And drivin' that way we crashed.
14. I couldn't I wasn't doin' nothin'. He was doin' it.

Statement #4 (Oral):
1. He (Miller) then got into the car and sat in the driver's seat. He (Miller) then started the car.
2. Rodney then got into the car and sat on top of him in the driver's seat.
3. He (Miller) put the car in gear.
4. He (Miller) was seated underneath Rodney in the driver's seat and Rodney was doing the gas and steering.
5. They drove like this for approximately one mile and hit the barbed wire fence. This happened because they

were going down the road and swerving around a short corner.
6. He (Miller) hit the brake at which point the car hit the barbed wire fence.

Statement #7 (Taped):
1. I put the car in drive. Rodney ran around to the passenger's side. He set in the car. I pulled off.
2. Synopsis: Miller states he drove the vehicle while Basu dragged from the car.

TOPIC: Who removed the baby from the BMW?
Statement #2 (Oral):
1. Rodney stopped the car because the baby was cryin'. Rodney took the whole child seat out the car.
2. Rodney took the baby out of the door behind him (Miller), which was the rear passenger's side door.
3. Rodney set the seat on the ground/grass and pulled off.

Statement #3 (Taped):
1. He pulled off; the baby was in the backseat cryin'. Then he took… He ran to the other side and pushed the baby in the grass—set the baby in the grass and he started… He drove off.

Statement #4 (Oral):
1. After they pulled off, Rodney stopped the car at which point he (Rodney) took the baby out of the car.

Statement #7 (Taped):
1. Rodney unhooked the seatbelt. I tossed the baby out of the car.

TOPIC: When was the baby removed from the BMW?
Statement #2 (Oral):
1. They drove a little ways before they took the baby out of the car. (Chronologically after Rodney pulled off real fast and hit something).
2. The baby was inside the car cryin'. Rodney drove a little bit and then snatched the baby out and put it down

on the side of the road. (Chronologically after Miller described Solomon releasing Pam Basu from the seatbelt).

Statement #3 (Taped):
1. We stopped the car. He snatched the lady off and the baby was cryin' in the backseat.
2. He snatched the lady. He let her go. She was still layin' right there.
3. He pulled off. The baby was in the backseat cryin'. Then he took—he ran on the other side and pushed the baby in the grass, set the baby in the grass and he started... He drove off.

Statement #4 (Oral):
1. The baby was still with them in the car when they hit the fence and the baby was crying.
2. After they pulled off Rodney stopped the car at which point he (Rodney) took the baby out of the car.

Statement #5 (Taped):
1. Synopsis: Miller first states that Rodney stopped the car and got out of the driver's door. Miller then changes the story and states that when Rodney stopped the car Rodney got out through the passenger's side door after crawling over Miller. He said this happened after they hit the fence.

Statement #7 (Taped):
1. Miller states that the baby was removed from the car before they hit the fence.

TOPIC: Where was Miller when the BMW was stolen from Pam Basu?

Statement #2 (Oral):
1. Rodney then pulled around the corner and said, 'Get in.'
2. When Rodney pulled up to him, Rodney was rushing him to get in the car by saying, 'Get in. Get in.'

3. He (Miller) was standing at the front passenger's side of the BMW when Rodney approached and grabbed the lady.

Statement #3 (Taped):
1. I was on the other side of the house. He pulled around saying, 'Get in.'
2. I was waitin' for him. Next thing I know he pulled around and said, 'Get in.'
3. Then he came around the corner. I got in the car.
4. Question: So you all went up to the car, Rodney grabbed her out of the car, right? Is that right?
   Answer: Uh huh.
5. Question: And when he grabbed her out of the car, you got in the driver's seat?
   Answer: Uh huh.

Statement #4 (Oral)
1. When Rodney went up to the lady with the BMW he (Miller) went right up with Rodney.

Statement #5 (Taped):
1. Questions: You and Rodney went up to the car together, is that right?
   Answer: Yes.

TOPIC: Was Pam Basu in or out of the car when she was approached by Solomon?

Statement #2 (Oral):
1. Rodney went up to the woman with the BMW and was standin' at the driver side of the car with her.

Statement #3 (Taped):
1. She was standin', she was standin' on the outside of the car.
2. And then, yeah, he tried to… He snatched her out. She was still had the seatbelt on.
3. Question: She was in the car?
   Answer: Yeah.

Statement #4 (Oral):
1. Rodney went up to the car and opened the door of the car.
2. Then Rodney snatched her. Rodney grabbed her arm. One of her arms was stuck in the seatbelt.

Statement #5 (Taped):
1. Rodney, Rodney forced—tried to take the lady out her car.

Statement #7 (Taped):
1. Rodney forcefully grabbed the lady by her neck.
2. He said get out the damn car.
3. He grabbed her by the throat.
4. He pulled her out of the car.

TOPIC: Location of Miller when Solomon approached Pam Basu

Statement #2 (Oral):
1. He and Rodney were standing at a corner on the other side of the house.
2. He (Miller) was standing at the front passenger's side of the BMW when Rodney approached and grabbed the lady.

Statement #3 (Taped):
1. I was standin' on the other side of the house.
2. Yes, I was standin' around the other side waitin' for him.
3. Question: So you all went up to the car, Rodney grabbed her out of the car, right? Is that right?
   Answer: Uh huh.
4. Question: And when he grabbed her out of the car, you got in the driver's seat?
   Answer: Uh huh.

Statement #4 (Oral):
1. When Rodney went up to the lady with the BMW he (Miller) went right up with Rodney.

Statement #5 (Taped):
1. Question: You and Rodney went up to the car together, is that right?
   Answer: Yes.

Statement #7 (Taped):
1. Me and Rodney waited for the lady at the Stop sign.
2. She looked at Rodney. Rodney forcefully grabbed the lady by her neck. I got in the car, started the car up. Put the car in drive.

TOPIC: Miller's seating location when the BMW is initially stolen.

Statement #2 (Oral):
1. The baby was in back of him (Miller) on the passenger's side rear seat.
2. Rodney took the baby out of the door behind him (Miller), which was the rear passenger's side door.
3. Rodney asked him to help get the seatbelt off of her body, but he (Miller) refused and stayed on the passenger's side.

Statement #3 (Taped):
1. Question: Okay, so then you got in the car and did you crawl into the front passenger's seat?
   Answer: Yeah.
2. Question: And when he grabbed her out of the car, you got in the driver's seat?
   Answer: Uh huh.

Statement #4 (Oral):
1. He (Miller) then got into the car and sat in the driver's seat.

TOPIC: Who was driving when the BMW struck the metal fence?

Statement #2 (Oral):
1. Rodney pulled off real fast and hit something.

Statement #3 (Taped):

1. We crashed the car when Rodney was tryin' to get me out of the seat.
2. Question: And when you hit the fence, who was driving?
   Answer: Me.
3. Question: Okay, and where was Rodney?
   Answer: On top of me, pushin' me out of the way.
4. I wasn't holdin' the steering wheel. I was just havin' my feet on the gas pedal.
5. I couldn't... I wasn't doin' nothin'. He was doin' it.

Statement #4 (Oral):
1. He (Miller) then got into the car and sat in the driver's seat. He (Miller started the car.
2. Rodney got into the car and sat on top of him in the driver's seat.
3. Miller put the car in gear.
4. Miller was seated underneath Rodney in the driver's seat and Rodney was doing the gas and steering.
5. They drove like this for approximately one mile and hit the fence. This happened because they were going down the road and swerving around a short corner.
6. He (Miller) hit the brake at which point the car hit the barbed wire fence.

Statement #7 (Oral):
1. Synopsis: Miller stated he was driving when they hit the fence.

TOPIC: When did Miller initially know that Pam Basu was being dragged alongside the vehicle?

Statement #2 (Oral):
1. He (Miller) did not see the lady fall when the car pulled off.
2. As they were driving he could smell and odor, remarking, "Flesh stinks." He smelled the bad odor from the beginning when they first took off in the

BMW. He said something to Rodney at which point Rodney stopped the car in the road. Rodney opened the door and he (Miller) saw the lady lying right there next to the car.

3. They knew the lady was dragging the entire time.

Statement #3 (Taped):

1. I got in the car then I started smellin' this little odor. We stopped the car and the lady was hangin', she was layin' on the ground with the seatbelt hooked to her left arm.
2. He drove off and yanked her.
3. I got—climbed into the driver's side on to the other side. Me and him was tanglin' up with each other. I saw the lady.
4. I didn't know she was still hooked on to the car, right?
5. Then he pushed me over and pulled off with the lady still—she was still hung up in there.
6. Question: You could see her hung up in there?
   Answer: Yeah. And I just started smellin'.

Statement #4 (Oral):

1. Then Rodney snatched her. Rodney grabbed her arm. One of her arms was stuck in the seatbelt.
2. Miller could see that her arm was stuck in the seatbelt.
3. Rodney then slammed on the gas pedal. Miller could see that the lady was still hooked to the car when Rodney did this.

Statement #5 (Taped):

1. Her arm was hooked to the seatbelt.
2. Rodney slammed on the gas pedal.
3. He was steering the car down the street, draggin' the lady.

Statement #7 (Taped):

1. She was hooked on the seatbelt.

2. Question: Now, when you closed the door, the lady's arm was caught in the seatbelt outside the door, right?
Answer: Her—her left arm was caught in the seatbelt.

TOPIC: Was the BMW car door open or closed when Pam Basu was approached?

Statement #3 (Taped):
1. It was open.

Statement #4 (Oral):
1. Rodney went up to the car and opened the door.

Statement #5 (Taped):
1. Question: Okay, and was the car door opened or closed?
Answer: Open.

Statement #7 (Taped):
1. The lady opened up the car door.
2. Rodney opened up the car door.

TOPIC: Pam Basu's action while the BMW was being stolen.

Statement #3 (Taped):
1. Yeah, she say 'Help. Help.'
2. She ain't sayin'… She wasn't sayin' nothin'.
3. She was unconscious. She wasn't sayin' nothin'.
4. Question: When you and Rodney went up to the car and Rodney grabbed the woman and was choking her and you got in and started the car, what was the woman saying?
Answer: Help.
5. She was screamin'.

Statement #5 (Taped):
1. Question: He slammed her out of the car? Was he wrestling with her?
Answer: Yes.

Statement #7 (Taped):
1. She was strugglin' with Rodney.

Fatal Destiny

2. Question: Okay, was she saying anything?
   Answer: No, she was just shocked.
3. Question: When you first closed the door, what was she doing while the car was still?
   Answer: She wasn't doin' nothin'. She was just layin' down. Her head face down, butt up.

TOPIC: Which car door did Miller originally use to enter the BMW?

Statement #2 (Oral):
1. Miller got in the BMW through the front passenger's door.

Statement #3 (Taped):
1. I got—climbed into the driver's side on to the other side.
2. Question: So, when you first got in the car, you got in through the driver's side in the rear door? Right?
   Answer: Yes.

TOPIC: Who originally closed the BMW's driver's door trapping Pam Basu in her seatbelt?

Statement #2 (Oral):
1. Rodney had the door shut and she was hooked outside the door.
2. Rodney got into the car and slammed the door.

Statement #3 (Taped):
1. Rodney grabbed the lady.
2. Choked her, slammed the car door and pulled off with the lady. And drove off with the lady in the car.

Statement #4 (Oral):
1. Rodney closed the car door, which slammed her arm in the door.

Statement #7 (Taped):
1. Question: Okay, and did you close the driver's door?
   Answer: Yes.

TOPIC: Where was the BMW when they originally approached it?
Statement #2 (Oral):
1. He and Rodney were standing at a corner on the other side of the house.
Statement #4 (Oral):
1. At the end of the townhouses. The car was parked with a little baby in the backseat.
Statement #5 (Taped):
1. Parked on the side near the sidewalk.
2. Question: Okay, and was it right in front of the house, right in front of the townhouse?
Answer: Yes.
Statement #7 (Taped):
1. Me and Rodney waited for the lady at the Stop sign.
TOPIC: Who drove off from the fence and where were they seated?
Statement #3 (Taped):
1. Then I said, Rodney pull off. He was drivin' from there. He said he was tryin' to get to the main highway.
Statement #4 (Oral):
1. Rodney closed the door and he (Miller) moved to the passenger's side.
2. Rodney backed the car up and pulled off, still dragging the victim.
Statement #7 (Taped):
1. I closed the driver's door.
2. Yes, I backed up.
TOPIC: How did Miller get the blood on his clothing?
Statement #2 (Oral):
1. Miller made no mention of blood on his clothing.
Statement #3 (Taped):

1. Only see because my clothes had the blood on them or somethin' 'cause he was sittin' on top of me and that lady was shut in the door.
2. Plus all three of us was in the one seat.
3. Plus she was shut in the door. Her left arm was shut and I had blood on my...
4. Question: Was her left arm actually inside the door?
   Answer: Yeah. It was shut in the seatbelt.
5. Question: So, you were rubbing up against it"
   Answer: Yeah.

Statement #4 (Oral):
1. He (Miller) got blood on his shirt when they were riding down the road and he was underneath Rodney. The window was down and the blood from the lady was blowing in the window on to him.
2. Rodney got blood from the lady on his hand when he shook her loose. When he (Miller) took his shirt off; Rodney wiped the blood off on Miller's shirt.

Statement #7 (Taped):
1. Question: Okay, and when you got out of the car, did you brush up against the body?
   Answer: Yes.
2. Question: And did you get blood on you?
   Answer: Yes.
3. Question: Did you brush up against her then?
   Answer: I brushed up against her.
4. Question: And you got more blood on you?
   Answer: Yes.

TOPIC: Who threw Miller's clothing from the vehicle?

Statement #2 (Oral):
1. Not mentioned.

Statement #3 (Taped):
1. Rodney threw them out the window.

2. Question: What part of your clothing did he throw out the window?
Answer: My pants.

Statement #4 (Oral):
1. Rodney threw his (Miller's) shirt out of the window.
2. He (Miller) took his pants off and threw them out of the window.

TOPIC: What happened when Solomon approached Pam Basu?

Statement #1 (Oral):
1. Rodney grabbed the lady.
2. Rodney took the car.
3. He told me to get in.

Statement #2 (Oral):
1. Rodney went up to the woman with the BMW and was standing at the driver's side door of the car with her.
2. While he was talking to her he pushed her out of the way and got into the BMW.
3. Rodney grabbed the lady when he first approached the car.

Statement #3 (Taped):
1. Rodney grabbed the lady.
2. Choked her. Slammed the car door and pulled of with the lady and drove off with the lady in the car.
3. She was standin'—she was standin' on the outside of the car.
4. And then, yeah, he tried to... He snatched her out. She was still had the seatbelt on.

Statement #4 (Oral):
1. Rodney went up to the car and opened the door of the car.
2. Then Rodney snatched her. Rodney grabbed her arm. One of her arms was stuck in the seatbelt.

Statement #5 (Taped):

1. Question: Okay, and was the car door opened or closed?
   Answer: Open.
2. Rodney, Rodney forced—tired to take the lady out her car.
3. Rodney grabbed the lady and I set in the car.
4. Rodney dragged her out of the car.
5. He just set her there. He slammed her. He slammed the lady out the car.
6. Question: Did Rodney choke her?
   Answer: Yes.

Statement #7 (Taped):
1. He opened the driver's side door.
2. He said get out the damn car.
3. He grabbed her by the throat.
4. He pulled her out of the car.
5. She was hooked to the seatbelt.
6. She was strugglin' with Rodney.

TOPIC: Discussion of committing a robbery prior to reaching the truck stop.

Statement #2 (Oral):
1. Not mentioned.

Statement #3 (Taped):
1. Rodney told me he was goin' to get a ride.

Statement #4 (Oral):
1. While walking to the rest area, Rodney told him he was about to go hard for a car, which meant that Rodney was going to try to wrestle someone's car from them by force.

Statement #5 (Taped):
1. Question: Okay, and what did Rodney tell you on the way to the rest area?
   Answer: He was gonna get another car.

2. Question: And how did he say he was going to get the car?
   Answer: He was gonna rough it off.
3. He was gonna forcibly take it from somebody.

Statement #7 (Taped):
1. After they reached the rest area Rodney said he was gonna get another car.
2. He was gonna rough somebody's car off.

TOPIC: Actions at the truck stop (rest area).

Statement #2 (Oral):
1. The trucks were locked. From the truck stop he and Rodney walked to some townhouses.

Statement #3 (Taped):
1. He went to the vending machine to use the phone.

Statement #4 (Oral):
1. When they arrived at the rest stop Rodney told him, 'Stand over here, I'm gonna try to get this car right here.
2. I was standin' waitin' for Rodney, lookin' around, waitin' for the police.
3. Then that's when we saw another lady at the car.
4. Rodney say he's gonna try to take her keys forcefully.
5. He, he—the lady hollered for help. Then that's when me and Rodney took off runnin'.

TOPIC: First person approached after Solomon and Miller ran out of gas.

Statement #2 (Oral):
1. They first went up to a lady and asked if they could use the phone.
2. This lady was a White female, approximately 24 years of age with a four-year-old child. She was outside near her vehicle, which was a burgundy Caravan.

Statement #3 (Taped):

1. First we saw a lady; we asked her if we could use the phone.
2. She had a baby in a Caravan—a burgundy Caravan.

Statement #4 (Oral):
1. Rodney approached a little 4 door vehicle and tried to take the car from a tall light skinned man. Rodney tried to pull the man out of the car.

TOPIC: Locating Pam Basu and the BMW.

Statement #2 (Oral):
1. They walked around toward another townhouse and saw a lady with a BMW. He and Rodney were standing at a corner on the other side of the house.

Statement #3 (Taped):
1. Went down the street to some townhouse. We saw a champagne—burgundy--um, brown BMW.

Statement #4 (Oral):
1. He and Rodney ran between some woods and into a townhouse development where they saw the lady at the end of the townhouses.

Statement #7 (Taped):
1. So we ran up the street. Ran through some townhouses. We spotted a brown BMW where a lady was loading the baby in the car seat.

TOPIC: Discussion of robbing Pam Basu prior to the robbery and murder.

Statement #2 (Oral):
1. Not mentioned.

Statement #3 (Taped):
1. Rodney say he was gonna come around. He said, 'I'm a see if I can get the car from the lady.'
2. He said, 'wait right here.' He say, 'I'm gonna,' he say, 'I'm gonna take the car from her.

Statement #5 (Taped):

1. Then he said he was gonna rough off another car. Then that's when we saw a brown BMW.
2. He was gonna tussle her for the car. Forcefully.

Statement #7 (Taped):
1. He just said he was gonna rough her off. He said this time we gonna get this car. He said this is the only car we could get.
2. He told me that he was gonna take the lady out the car and I was gonna drive.

Appendix B

Appendix B will provide definitions and terminology connected with Forensic Science tests. Michael Marinaro of the Maryland State Police Crime Laboratory provided the information contained herein.

Forensic Science: The application of the natural sciences to matters of law. It includes a variety of different activities and specialties. In practice, forensic science draws upon the principles and methods of all the traditional sciences, such as physics, chemistry and biology.

Forensic Serology: The examination of all body fluid evidence. Forensic serologists conduct examinations of suspected body fluids in order to:
1. Identify the fluid.
2. Establish if it is of human origin.
3. Try to associate the fluid with particular individuals as possible sources.

Identification of Blood:
    A. Phenolphthalein Test: This is the oxidative test for the presumptive identification of blood based on the catalytic activity of the heme group of hemoglobin. This test is extremely sensitive and a detection of as little as one part blood in one million parts water can be made.
    B. Luminol Test: Hemoglobin enhancement of luminol luminescence subsequent to its alkaline oxidation provides a test for the identification of blood. Use of the luminol test is when the presence of blood is suspected, but not visible.

Blood Groups – Genetic Markers.

A. ABO System: ABO is the best known of the blood group systems based on its importance in matching blood transfusions. The ABO System is based on antigens and antibodies.
   1. Antibody: An immunoglobulin molecule with specific receptor sites formed in response to an antigenic stimulus. The term is usually used collectively to refer to molecules with similar specificity with a serum specimen.
   2. Antigen: Any substance, which can stimulate neutralizing antibody production when introduced into a host body.
B. ABO
   1. Group O – 45%
   2. Group A – 40%
   3. Group B – 10%
   4. Group AB – 5%
C. Enzyme: The protein substance produced by living cells capable of speeding up specific chemical transformations, such as hydrolysis, oxidation, or reduction, but is unaltered itself in the process, a biological catalyst.
D. Genetic Marker: A readily recognizable gene, which can be used in family and population studies.
E. Genetic Markers:
   1. EsD   =   Esterase D
   2. PGM =   Phosphoglucomutase
   3. GLOI =   Glyoxalase I
   4. EAP =   Erythrocyte Acid Phosphatase
   5. ADA =   Adenosine Deaminase
   6. AK   =   Adenylate Kinase

7. PepA = Peptidase A
8. CAII = Carbonic Anhydrase II
F. Lewis System: Used for determination of secretor status.
1. Secretor: An individual whose secretions (especially saliva) contain water-soluble A, B and H substances.
2. Non-secretor: One who does not have water-soluble A, B and H substances in his secretions.

The following information relates to the drug screening process used to determine the concentration of controlled dangerous substances in the urine samples obtained from Bernard Eric Miller and Rodney Eugene Solomon. Charles Lodcio of the National Center for Forensic Science provided the data.

ng = nanogram
mL = milliliter

Nano in its combined form means one billionth of a part; in this case nanogram refers to one billionth of a part of a gram per milliliter of fluid.

Note: The samples obtained from Miller and Solomon were taken three days after their arrests. According to Mr. Lodico the readings would have been much higher if the samples were obtained on the day of the incident.

About the Author

James Lilley is a former Marine and highly decorated, twenty-five year veteran of the Howard County, Maryland Police Department. His awards included the Medal of Valor, four Bronze Stars, four Unit Citations and the governor's citation. Jim was selected as the Police-Writers.com 2008 Author of the Year, has written articles for Police Chief Magazine, the International Association of Chief's of Police and has penned seven novels. In August 2011, Sensei Takeshi Miyagi promoted Mr. Lilley to 9th Degree Black Belt in Shorin Ryu Karate Do.

www.ingramcontent.com/pod-product-compliance
Lightning Source LLC
Chambersburg PA
CBHW041429300426
44114CB00002B/8